WRITERS REPUBLIC

SACRED
BLISTERS

A PILGRIM'S LOOK AT THE HISTORY, MYSTERY & LIFE LESSONS LEARNED
ON **EL CAMINO DE SANTIAGO**

STEVE WALTHER

FOREWORD BY DAN MULLINS

WRITERS REPUBLIC L.L.C.
515 Summit Ave. Unit R1
Union City, NJ 07087, USA

Website: *www.writersrepublic.com*
Hotline: *1-877-656-6838*
Email: *info@writersrepublic.com*

Ordering Information:
Quantity sales. Special discounts are available on quantity purchases by corporations, associations, and others. For details, contact the publisher at the address above.

Library of Congress Control Number:		2023900261	
ISBN-13:	979-8-88810-454-5	[Paperback Edition]
	979-8-88810-455-2	[Hardback Edition]
	979-8-88810-456-9	[Digital Edition]

Rev. date: 01/04/2023

Contents

Foreword for Sacred Blisters

Pilgrimage is about new beginnings.

We walk out our door to explore another part of the world. We travel in slow motion, providing our heart and soul with space to soar. You may be one of millions of pilgrims who have walked el Camino de Santiago, full of the spirit of the saint in whose name you walk, St James the Stronger. You might have walked the Portuguese route, the Norte, Primitivo or Camino Madrid. One thing is certain, you would have surprised yourself with your capability to explore the landscape and culture - and your inner you.

I host My Camino - the Podcast - a weekly interview with a pilgrim from somewhere around the world, someone hoping to share their wisdom and in doing so, making some sense of the essence of their journey for themselves. I first interviewed Steve Walther back in April 2019. He had just returned from the Camino and was basking in the glow of spiritual journey. I said at the time the discussion didn't sound or feel like an interview, it felt more like two 50+ men having a chat at a bar in Spain. We're kindred spirits in many ways, our stories twist and turn like shoelaces on a pilgrim's boot. Steve and I share a love of family, our communities, sports and el Camino.

The Camino can provide respite for a troubled soul, a gentle reminder of what's important, or guidance for a restless spirit. You'll find yourself walking with strangers who become friends, you'll tell stories you wouldn't tell even your closest friends, and you'll listen to stories that will astonish and inspire you. Your feet carry you but your heart leads you. Your mind is happy to be led by the whispering of your inner self. What a joy. What a blessing.

You're about to be taken on a journey through soaring pines and creeping vines. Sacred Blisters takes us through cobbled town squares while church bells ring in the distance. You'll skin your knees, you'll sleep within reach of complete strangers and marvel at the din of snorers in perfect harmony. You'll learn about the history of the Camino, the culture of those who live along the ancient trail, and why it resonates with pilgrims all around the world. Sacred Blisters is both a guidebook and a book to use as a guide. You'll be led and you may even learn to lead.

Enjoy the ups and downs of Steve's Camino, sacred blisters and all. Most of all, enjoy his new beginnings. You may find yourself walking the very same trails, returning home with a glow to warm those you love.

I hope you find what you're looking for somewhere along the Way

Buen Camino

Dan Mullins
Sydney, Australia
December 2022

Introduction

If you are reading this book, you have most likely heard something about El Camino de Santiago de Compostela. If you are wanting to learn more about the Camino, my intent in sharing my experiences is to motivate you to take your first step onto the Way of St. James.

For those that know the sound of gravel crunching beneath your boots keeping time with the rhythm of the clicking walking sticks and church bells chiming in the distance, then my hope is to remind you of that special feeling that one can get only while on the pilgrimage to Santiago. With my experiences, stories, and lessons learned on the Camino, I know your own memories and emotions will bring smiles, tears, and a warmed heart.

Once the Camino de Santiago is in you, you are changed forever. The history, mystery, culture, food, local people, and, most importantly, the pilgrims all come together to create something beyond place. El Camino is not just a trail, and the pilgrimage is far more than a hike. Some walk for religious reasons or to seek spiritual answers. Others walk to mourn the loss of loved ones. I met many pilgrims that set off seeking an adventurous physical challenge and came home realizing that perhaps the mental challenge was both a more daunting and fulfilling task.

For whatever one's reasons are for taking their first step onto the Camino, their journey really begins upon their return home. Life lessons learned on the Camino changed my perspective of my own journey through life. I learned patience. I gained faith in my fellow human beings. People are inherently good, and the Camino is the perfect venue that reminds people of this and launches them back into the world with a newfound want to help, need to give, care, and make those around them want to be better people. It is contagious!

This book is not a self-help book. Nor is it a story of overcoming adversity or an attempt to persuade people to live or think a certain way. This is my story of finding my own path and how I learned to live my life in the most happy and loving way I can. A path that, with each step on and off the Camino, I am striving to be the best version of myself.

I want to share my history as it pertains to how the Camino changed my perspective and path in life. I also want to dive into the history of St. James and how he came to rest on the side of a hill in rural Galicia, Spain. And what that has meant to the people of Spain and the millions of pilgrims that have been making the journey for over a thousand years. And last but not least, I want to share my stories of life lessons learned on the Camino and the lifelong friends from around the world that have come into my life because of the man that went on a walk across the Iberian Peninsula two centuries ago. I have walked alongside some of these pilgrims, while others, connected via Camino-themed podcasts and websites. But one thing that is for sure is that once you've experienced the magic that is abundant on Camino, you have a connection that bonds you to all those that have ever walked on the Way of St. James.

Chapter

1

Jimmy, Don't I Know Your Name?

Before I get hate mail from those that think I am making light of the religious importance of St. James, I want to be very clear that I am not. I have been a lifelong Catholic, and was even an altar boy for a time growing up. I was married in the Cathedral of Jerez de la Frontera, Cadiz, Spain. I am proud of the good that the church has had in my family's lives and for so many people in need.

With that said, certainly some of the recent bad actors inside of the church and the negative perception have made anything religious somewhat taboo to talk about in many social situations. When thinking about religion in the twenty-first century, I turn to something I heard Father Len MacMillan say in Mass many years ago: "The Church is run by people, human beings. People are not perfect. The lessons in Jesus's teachings are perfect. Don't get hung up in the delivery or the rules made by people; but rather take to heart the words that Jesus himself gave us. The rest really isn't that important."

This single message changed my perception of religion today. I realized that the various offshoots of Christianity have forgotten the core of the religion and placed man-made ritual and procedure above the actual message of Christ. That message was really quite simple and focused on these three basic principles: Love God. Love thy neighbor. Love thy self. It really isn't that complicated!

Whether you believe in God or not, that is up to you. If you are not a Christian, I can love you as equally as I love those that are. If truth be told, some of the most unchristian people I have met have worn their religion on their sleeves. I have actually met Atheists, Buddhists, Muslims, Hindus and Jews on the Camino. All were there for the same reason: looking for answers to life's challenges and uncertainties.

So, with that out of the way, let's dive into the story of St. James and how he became the guy that started this two-thousand-year-old walkabout. First off, let's start with his name itself. James has a lot of "also known as" names. Since I am writing this in English, we'll start with "James." In the Bible, he is known as "James the Great," also known as James, son of Zebedee. "The Great" or "Greater" moniker is due to his age compared to the other apostle, James the Lesser. I've read that James the Greater was both older and taller. Jesus called both of the apostles named James "Yakob." "Yakob" and "Jacob" are both the same as James in Hebrew. Connected to this particular name for St. James, the French route of the Camino is often referred to as the "Jacobean" route. In the language of Galicia, where he now is interned, his name is Xacobo. In Portuguese, St. James is known as Tiago." And in Spanish, James comes in two forms, "Jacobo" and "Santiago." (I am not sure where the modern name "Jaime" fits into the James narrative.)

I'm getting a little *ahead* of myself in the story, but one of the most interesting names for St. James was bestowed upon him over eight hundred years after he lost his head. In the legend of the Battle of Clavijo, in modern-day Asturias, fought between the Christians and Muslims in the year 844, St. James miraculously appeared to lead the outnumbered Christian Spaniards to defeat the much larger Muslim army. Riding a white horse with raised sword in hand and wearing a scallop shell on his hat, St. James led the Spaniards into battle. The Christians were victorious, and the name "Matamoros" was given to James (Moor-Slayer). Scholars debate whether this battle actually happened, but nonetheless, at the time, it was used as a rallying cry for the Christians against the Muslims' push north through the Iberian Peninsula. After this battle, real or fabricated, St. James was made the patron saint of Spain and affectionately referred to as El Matamoros. Something that seems to have slipped by the scope of today's PC police!

On my first trip to Santiago decades before I made my first pilgrimage, the only souvenir I purchased was a bottle opener. The opener had a figure of St. James atop his white steed, raised sword on one end and a bottle opener on the other. At the time I purchased this treasure, I had no idea of its significance. But when I am asked to open a bottle for somebody today, whether they want to hear it or not, the opened bottle comes with a story!

I travel for work and often find myself at the far southern tip of Texas at the US–Mexico border near Brownsville. The town on the Mexican side of the border is named "Matamoros." Knowing what I know about St. James and the name "Matamoros," I have asked many people that live in that region if they know what it means and the origin of the name. To date, nobody has been able to answer the question. They can figure out what it means by translating but have no idea of the context.

The Cathedral in Santiago de Compostela

3

Santiago, Fall

So now let's talk about the name of this pilgrimage itself. Depending on where you are, with whom you are speaking, and in what context, the Camino has many different names. The most common and widely accepted is "El Camino de Santiago de Compostela." Which in English translates to "the Way of St. James under a field of stars." The "field of stars" part is credited to the place where St. James was discovered in a Roman sepulcher in the ninth century.

The name is often shortened to "El Camino." Which when translated into English means "the Way." This is another really interesting part of the lore and one of the really powerful things that makes the Camino even more special. In the early days of Christianity, "the Way" was used in connection with followers of Christ. "The Way" is mentioned several times in the book of Acts. The Romans even referred to "the Way" as a sect of Judaism rather than a separate religion. And last but not least, the famous Bible passage, "Jesus said to him, 'I am THE WAY, the truth, and the life. No one comes to the father except through me'" (John 14:6). I am not one to regularly quote the Bible ... I promise to keep it to a minimum before I start losing readers! But I do think that "the Way" aspect of "El Camino" is not known by most pilgrims and something particularly important and fascinating to point out.

Chapter

2

Life Lessons: No Matter How Difficult Things Seem, Someone Is Succeeding with Far Less

Preparing for my first pilgrimage in the fall of 2018, I read all that I could about what to wear, what kind of shoes and socks were the best, which backpack was the lightest, poles or no poles, and all the way down to the best underwear for the Camino. I studied maps, worked out the daily potential stops, sites, villages, history—all the information I could gobble up. I later learned from podcaster great Dan Mullins that my condition is known as a "spreadsheet" pilgrim. I am what I am…

With my pre-Camino preparation, I came across an article written by a Camino veteran that stated that to cut down on weight, no need to bring a flashlight because if you are with a smart phone, you already are equipped with a very bright flashlight. This made a lot of sense, so one of the first items in the bag came out of the bag!

The first part of my Camino experience exceeded all expectations and was even more than I had hoped. Coming into the cathedral to the sounds of bagpipes and pure elation of all that had entered the city that day is an emotion shared with only those that have lived it. This was late fall, and the days were cool. We experienced a few sprinkles in the days leading into Santiago, but nothing too bad, and because of the cool days, we really never had to set out on the daily walk in the early

6

morning predawn like pilgrims do when walking in the midsummer months to beat the heat.

After Santiago, I continued my pilgrimage to Finisterre. As I mentioned prior, the bagpipes greeted me on my entry into the magical city; however, a hard-pounding rain showed me to the door as I walked out of the city center and up the first hill toward my first stop on the way to the coast. Even though it rained for most of the day, the rhythm of my boots on the wet trail and the sound of rain dripping from the trees and the raised water flowing through the gullies and streams made for a change of scenery accompanied by an orchestra of nature. I had entered the city with my first Camino family and now left them as they prepared to leave for their journeys home. My first walk out of Santiago was alone and in the rain.

I left Santiago late that morning and arrived soaked and cold, but in good spirits. I stayed that night in a three-hundred-year-old home in Negreira called Casa de Bola. A young man checked me into the house. He shared that he was born in the house, as was his father and grandfather. His father had passed, and now he and his mother ran the boardinghouse. The house and the room were incredible and, most importantly, out of the rain. In the morning, my clothes had dried and my demeanor had warmed. In an attempt to make up for my shortened day prior, I set out on the Camino a couple of hours before the first signs of daylight. I headed out of the house armed with my rain jacket, poncho, and trusty smart phone flashlight.

Minutes into my early walk, the rain started. The path led into a very dark forest. As the rain turned from a drizzle to the bucket variety, I quickly realized that the "Camino veteran" had obviously never walked at night in the rain on a dark forest trail using his smart phone! The phone's screen became wet, which meant that using the touch screen had no effect in moving the cursor. Fears of my phone becoming too wet and sparks flying as it fizzled overcame me. I had everything on that phone. My itinerary for my flight home, my spreadsheet notes on where I was going to stay and stops yet to come. With this anxiety of the phone succumbing to the elements, I dried it off the best I could with my shirt under my rain jacket and buried it deep inside of an inner pocket, and into the darkness I walked.

It was so dark that I walked by braille … with my arms out in front of me, feeling for the branches of the trees and bushes so that I could navigate and try to stay on the center of the trail.

At one point, the trail came to a "T." At the crossing point, I could see one of the Camino markers that line the Camino from beginning to end, typically placed at junctions or places where it may not be clear which direction the actual Camino leads. The markers usually include a yellow arrow indicating the direction of the Camino and the kilometers remaining, in this case to Finisterre. This marker was straight ahead and the choice was to go right or left. It was perched a bit elevated above the trail and I could make out the form of the marker, but not the direction in which the indented yellow arrow pointed. Peeping out of my poncho's hood, I stretched out over the small ditch with a river of rainwater gushing down the side of the trail, put my knee into the embankment and reached up over the mud to feel the "indented yellow arrow" on the marker to make certain I continued my march into darkness in, at the very least, the correct direction.

As I leaned forward, I heard a voice out of the darkness. The voice asked, "What in the hell are you doing?"

Thinking that I was alone in the dark without witnesses to my predicament, I sheepishly replied, "I don't have a light, and I can't see the arrow's direction …?"

The man's face, lit by his own headlamp, said more in his look than with any words after that. His look said, *Another dumbass American …* His actual words then followed as, "Uh … follow me …"

Juhwan's headlamp showing my lightless happiness

I gathered myself and quickly stepped in line behind the man and followed him through the forest, keeping close behind as to keep the branches from whacking me in the face. In fifteen minutes or so, the light began to make its way through the dark clouds and morning rain. I introduced myself to the young man and at the first village and I invited him to join me for the first café con leche of the morning.

His name was Juhwan Lee. He was a forty-one years old and from South Korea. He had started on Camino thirty-two days prior in Saint-Jean-Pied-de-Port walking the French Route of the Camino into Santiago and was now carrying on to Finisterre and Muxia. My brother lives and works in Korea and is married to a Korean, so we had a point of connection. He knew of the university where my brother worked, and we talked about life in Seoul and Eagle, Idaho. After coffee, we continued our walk back into the elements.

Juhwan and Steve

I asked Juhwan about his journey and of his experiences. His story was one that has stuck with me to this day. He said that he was changing jobs and had this time off before starting his new job. He read an article about the Camino and thought he may never have the opportunity to do it again, so he decided to take this trip while he had the break and time between jobs.

Juhwan

Juhwan said that he had never been on an airplane or left Korea before flying from Seoul to Paris. He said that he could speak some English, but no French or Spanish. He recounted his landing in Paris and the difficulties in navigating his way to the train station to find a train to Saint-Jean-Pied-de-Port. He eventually figured it out. But he was still alone and fearful to talk to other pilgrims due to his lack of language. He set out from Saint-Jean-Pied-de-Port alone and discouraged. The first day over the Pyrenees is a particularly long and hard walk up and over a mountain pass. He struggled and came to the decision that the next day, he would find a taxi back to Saint-Jean and head home.

My second Camino, armed with headlamp!

As he set out the next morning looking for a taxi or means of transportation, he met an elderly Korean man walking alone with a backpack, a walking stick, and a smile from ear to ear. He asked the man in Korean, "How old are you?"

The man replied that he was seventy-two. Juwan asked him how his journey was going so far.

The senior pilgrim said to him, "I am seventy-two years old. I have never been on an airplane. I've never left Korea. I was able to explore Paris and take the train to Saint-Jean-Pied-de-Port. I saw the most incredible views hiking up and over the Pyrenees and saw so many extraordinary people these first two days. I speak no Spanish, no French, and no English, but everybody is so helpful!

Juhwan then shared with me that the old man had changed his perspective in an instant. If this seventy-two-year-old that did not even have English as a fall back to communicate is succeeding on the Camino, he could also do it. He said that he never looked back and walked all the way to Santiago and decided to continue on to Finisterre and Muxia just because he could!

Juhwan's story is one that I often reflect back on feeling sorry for myself with regard to something that is happening at the time. Life is wonderful if you change your perspective. Challenging times usually last a moment in terms of the big picture.

No matter how difficult things seem, someone is succeeding with far less.

Chapter

3

St. James and His Kung Fu Grip

St. James

If I were a kid collecting "apostle action figures," James would be my guy! He's not one of the more famous apostles, and there are no rhyming sayings to remember his name, as in the famed "Mathew, Mark, Luke, and John, hold the horse while I get on!" James wasn't the great writer, orator, even a natural recruiter to the new Christian religion. But he did have swagger and a toughness that makes him my favorite of the twelve action figures!

To start with, James was a fisherman. That makes him tops in my book! I think people that fish have a unique natural blend of patience and the ability to figure things out. James was persistent. When questioning his faith during his long walkabout throughout the Iberian Peninsula, he had doubt. In the context of being a fisherman, he perhaps considered "cutting bait" and heading home.

I'm skipping a bit ahead in the story, but in the year AD 40, while sitting on the banks of the Ebro river near modern-day Zaragoza, James was discouraged at his lack of success in bringing Christianity to the region. At the very moment he was about to pull in the nets and row home, the Virgin Mary appeared to him. She reassured him that what he was doing was not in vain. And if you think about it, she was absolutely correct when considering how in just a short time after his journey, Christianity eventually spread across the entire peninsula.

Along with his younger brother, St. John the Apostle, they had the best "action figure" duo nickname of all of the apostle brother duos (interestingly, of the twelve apostles, there were three sets of brothers). Both Mark and Luke reference James and John as the Sons of Thunder because of their characteristic fiery zeal! Peter and Andrew were cool and all ... but they were no Sons of Thunder!

And regarding the swagger and toughness, James walked all over the Iberian Peninsula telling people about his "mystic savior" from back home that taught kindness, doing good, being good while simultaneously facing hatred, ill will, and evil. James was forced to be vigilant, dodging and weaving the very Romans that killed his teacher. He had to be cautious of bandits and Roman sympathizers that could potentially turn him in. He walked thousands of miles without today's luxuries like hiking boots, a rain jacket, a waterproof backpack/tent or freeze-dried snacks for his difficult journey. He faced ridicule and punishment each and every day. Yet he walked on. This sense of walking through adversity and pain is one of the things that all pilgrims experience as they walk the Way today.

Even though our path today is paved with well-marked yellow arrows, comfortable lodging, incredible coffee, inexpensive cuisine, and fine wine, there are still difficulties that demonstrate what this pilgrimage is really about.

Chapter

4

Turn Down That Racket!

Team "Turn Down That Racket", 2018

On my first Camino, I walked with a pair of wonderful Canadian peregrinas and a pilgrim from Brazil. We had walked together for several days when on this particular morning, we walked in silence. The morning sunrise put on an incredible show of colors with light pushing through a belt of fog. It was quite spectacular. The four of us stared in amazement on the first knoll that provided our very own balcony from which to watch the full display unfold.

"Pre-Racket Sunrise", 2018

We marched on in silence, each in our own thoughts. Then it started, very faint in the distance at first. Then the noise gradually got louder and louder. Over the next couple of kilometers, we each walked on, without a word between us, with only occasional glances back, waiting to see where this "racket" was coming from.

Then they appeared. First off, this wasn't just the ordinary kind of racket. This was the type that was the worst type of agony for those of us over fifty: *rap music*. Worse yet, Spanish rap music. The four of us all turned back at the same time to catch our first glimpse. Six teenaged Spanish boys in a long hiking queue spaced about two steps between them. The one in the back had a large Bluetooth speaker from which the noise blasted for all to "enjoy." The boys walked in time and rhythm to the rap music, as if they were marines marching in cadence to an early morning drill. As they gained on our smaller group, the music continued to get louder and louder. The four of us continued to get angrier and angrier, all the while without actually saying anything to each other.

I couldn't help but wonder how these boys could be disrespecting the Camino so much by playing this music so loud on this religious pilgrimage... So disrespectful!

By the looks on the faces of our group, it was very evident that we all shared the same thoughts of disbelief and horror.

And then it happened. The first boy passed us. He was a young high-school-aged boy. He was smiling from ear to ear, oozing happiness and joy. As he passed each of us, he said, "Buen Camino!" (the "greeting" of the Camino between pilgrims, which is Bom Camino in Portugal).

The second young man passed, also smiling the same eager, joyous happiness, and said, "Buen Camino!" to each of us as he marched past.

The third, fourth, fifth, and, finally, the sixth young pilgrim, each just as content and full of life as the one before him. Courteous and polite as they passed us old-timers, all with the same enthusiastic salutation, "Buen Camino!"

The four of us all paused after they passed. We all looked at each other, again, without a single word among us. *We all felt the same thing, and we all knew it.* Those boys were doing the Camino their way. We were doing it our way, while they were doing it their way. Neither way is better than the other. The fact that in this day and age these six teenagers were out doing something so significant was a beautiful thing. The fact that they were doing it to the beat of rap music was our problem, not theirs!

"The Turn down that Racket Crew"

At that very moment, I pointed up to the heavens and said to myself, *God, you tricky bugger! That was a great lesson. You got me!*

As this realization came over me, simultaneously, it struck the rest of my pilgrim family. We all knew what had just happened. The Camino taught us that there is no wrong way, just your way.

Enjoy the company of all pilgrims, all people, and from them, we can all learn new things and be happy in any situation. Life is wonderful, if you remember to enjoy and live it!

Chapter

5

You Can't Go Home Again
More History of St. James:
Walking, Boat Rides, and
an Eight-Hundred-Year
Game of Hide-and-Seek

Back to the history... After James received his encouragement from Mary with her famous pep talk on the banks of the Ebro, he continued to spread the word and share the story of Jesus. Finally, Christianity started to take foot and the number of followers grew. Sometime between the years forty-two and forty-four, James decided it was time to head back to Jerusalem to see what was happening with the other followers of Christ and the status of the Way. Upon his arrival, he was identified by the Romans and captured, and Herod ordered his head cut off. His return home only solidified the old saying, "You can't go home again!" This beheading made James the first martyr of Christianity.

Here is where the story becomes part history, part legend, and part mystery. Two of James's disciples, Theodore and Anastasius, wanted to bring him back to Galicia. They decided best to bury him near the magic and mystery of "Finis Terrae" (today called Finisterre/Fisterra), which was considered to be the end of the world at his time. They wrapped the body and head of James in cloth and sealed them inside of a box/

ark and loaded it into a small boat. They set off from Haifa, Palestine, for the northwest corner of the Iberian Peninsula. They landed near modern-day Padron.

Finisterre, End of the Earth with Sebastian & Evelyn

For those walking on the Portuguese Route, I encourage you to step into the Church of Santiago in Padron for a chance to see the Roman altar dedicated to the god Neptune. According to the legend, the boat carrying the remains of James was transferred from the boat to this very altar. Another side note regarding the town of Padron: if you are making the pilgrimage from there to Santiago, after getting the stamp from the Church of Santiago, you can also get a certificate from the parish as "proof" that you visited the sacred city of Padron and the place where St. James's body was brought to land on the voyage back from the Holy Lands.

I would certainly get mail from readers if I didn't also mention an interesting piece of the legend regarding the boat that delivered the body of St. James to Galicia. I have read that it was a small sailboat when it left Haifa, Palestine. But it is often described as a "stone boat without rudder and without sail" when it reached the shores of Galicia. One of the stories is that angels picked him up in a stone boat and sailed him back to Galicia. Sometimes you just have to go with the story and not question the validity of a "stone boat," how that would even work, or what it would look like. They call this trust *faith*!

Roman Altar dedicated to Neptune

Another interesting legend is that above the cliffs overlooking the estuary, a knight was riding a horse as the stone boat entered the river. Seeing the stone boat, the horse spooked and leapt into the cold water, with the knight still mounted on his steed (again, going back to the validity of the "stone boat" itself … a floating stone boat even freaked out a horse!). The legend tells of St. James's appearance and magically lifting the horse and rider from the water to the safety of the shore. Once on land, the horse and the knight were both covered in scallop shells. I have heard and read the same story with different variations of the same basic plot of horse-rider-ocean-miraculous lifeguarding by St. James-scallop shells. In these alternative stories, usually you can replace the knight with a bride or a groom on horseback headed to his wedding.

Since we drifted into the topic of scallop shells, let's touch on how they relate to the Camino. Beyond the aforementioned stone boat and St. James's lifting of the scallop-covered horse and rider/s from the sea, there are many aspects of the scallop shell that has made it one of the symbols of the Camino. Perhaps the most practical purposes of the scallop shell are that they were used by pilgrims to drink water from springs and streams. The other tie to the scallop shell and the Camino is the fact that scallops are very typical of the Galician coast, so the thought that pilgrims brought back scallop shells as souvenirs, or even proof that they made it all the way to Santiago, seems to be the most believable story.

Gallician Scallops

Back to the mooring of the stone boat in Padron. Upon landing ashore at the estuary of the Ulla and Sar rivers, near Iria Flavia, they transported his body overland about twenty kilometers to Compostela using an ox and a cart. There are many legends regarding the actual transfer of the Santiago's body, but they were written centuries after the event. So who knows for sure? We are going to assume for the sake of the story and the pilgrimage itself that he was brought to his current resting location and tucked away and hidden for the next eight centuries.

The Stone Boat

For those pilgrims that choose to do the Portuguese Route, whether the Coastal or Central Routes, I cannot recommend more to consider taking the Spiritual Variant option. When leaving Pontevedra, there is a fork in the Camino. To the right, the Camino leads to Padron. To the left is the Spiritual Variant, also known as the Traslatio Route, the Maritime Route, and the Arousa Sea Route.

What makes this option so incredibly special, especially for us history geeks, is that it actually follows the route made with the remains of St. James when coming back to the Iberian Peninsula in the stone boat, "led by an angel and guided by a star." St. James's body arrived on the coast of Galicia and sailed up the river Ulla until it reached Iria Flavia, now called Padron. It is considered to be the origin of all the Caminos de Santiago. The Spiritual Variant consists of three stages with an additional fourth stage consisting of the final walk in from Padron to Santiago de Compostela.

The first of the stage starts in Pontevedra. A beautiful walk passing through a few small villages and eucalyptus forests takes you to an incredible Benedictine monastery, Monasterio de San Xoan Poio (Monastery of St. John). It was founded in the seventh century during the Middle Ages and abandoned by the Benedictine monks in the early nineteenth century before being restored and occupied by the Order of La Merced. The monastery has an incredible museum and exhibit of Camino pieces and history, including an original copy of the Codex Calixtinus. Details on the importance of the Codex are described in a later chapter.

From the Monasterio de San Xoan Poio, the Camino takes you down to the fishing village of Combarro before climbing and climbing and climbing over a series of rural mountains and dropping into a small village with another beautiful monastery, Monasterio de Armenteira. Anybody making this stop must stay at the monastery itself and attend the pilgrims' blessing at 7:00 p.m. nightly. If you aren't staying there, you can still attend the blessing. For me and the pilgrims that I was walking with at the time, the stay at the monastery in Armenteira was one of the highlights of our entire Camino experience. The nuns performed prayers by singing in such an angelic delivery that moved the pilgrims to tears. The evening we were there, there were nine nuns, one priest, and only five pilgrims at the service. It was such a moving and wonderful experience that I wanted to know more about how these nuns came to live in this remote hidden stop far from anywhere. After the service, we met with the other pilgrims for dinner in a restaurant right outside the doors of the monastery. The five of us all shared that we had the same emotional response to the service and the same questions regarding the monastery's full-time residents.

The second stage consists of perhaps the most beautiful five kilometers that I have walked on any of the Caminos. From Armenteira to Pontearenlas, the Camino follows a cascading creek that flows through moss-covered trees and rocks. Probably the best description of this section would be that the forest was one in which you might imagine Robin Hood and Little John to be around each bend in the stream. Walking in the shade of the trees, several old water gristmills are resting on the banks of the tumbling water. This section of the Camino is called the Route of Stone and Water.

After the walk with Robin Hood, the Camino takes you through the Fento wine region. *Fento* means "fern" in Galician. Today there are many more grape vines than ferns. The Camino takes you right through many kilometers of vineyards. This sub-region of wine is unique because the micro-climates throughout this area provide several different tasting grapes/wines. The cool, damp climate from the Atlantic Ocean combined with warm dry areas that get very warm in the summer and the granite/slate soil creates the "stress" that is needed for the best wine grapes to thrive and create unique flavors found nowhere else. I visited with an old timer local in Armenteira and he told me that the Rias Baixas (lower river estuaries) region is really the garden of Eden. I had a hard time thinking of a reason to disagree with the man—all the way down to the wild fig trees growing along the Camino!

The Vilanova Spiritual Variant planning dinner

27

The Camino eventually drops back down to the ocean before arriving in the fishing village and port of Vilanova de Arousa. Here, pilgrims have two choices. They can continue walking the twenty-eight kilometers following the coastline to Padron or take a boat in which you will follow the actual waterway path that carried the body of Santiago with his two disciples, Theodore and Anastasius. Other than there not being a boat available at the time you are there, I'm not sure why anybody would "choose" to walk versus taking the historic boat ride.

Having completed this stage in November, we had three obstacles. The first being that it was far from peak season and there were very few pilgrims on this route. In the low season, there are few boats that operate and will not travel without full boats. Secondly, we arrived on a Sunday and had a difficult time contacting any of the boat companies or captains. And the third hurdle is that the boats can only navigate the estuary, which eventually turns into a riverway during the high tide. The timing of finding a boat and the tides makes the departure time very difficult to determine ahead of time. During the high season, the boat departure times are published on websites, and there are several boats available to purchase a seat.

We had a secret weapon—Ivy! Ivy was an incredible pilgrim from Taiwan. I will tell more Ivy stories in a later chapter, but Ivy and another wonderful Portuguese pilgrim, Sergio, and I walked together on the Spiritual Variant since leaving Pontevedra. Finding a boat captain and information regarding the nautical options was difficult as we made our way after the left fork onto the Spiritual Variant route. We were a bit nervous about our prospects of actually finding somebody to take us up the river. Ivy spoke English very well, but she did not speak any Spanish. She was very motivated and determined to find a captain. She searched the internet and brochures and asked every pilgrim that we met along the route what they knew about the boating situations. Armed with a few phone numbers, she initiated her attack. Along the Camino during the first two days and at each of our lunch and coffee stops, she was calling, texting, and emailing all the numbers that she could find.

In Armenteira, one of the other pilgrims that had attended the pilgrim blessing at the monastery joined us in the restaurant outside the gates for dinner. Juan Carlos, a Catalan, had walked in right at seven that night with another pilgrim named Bernard from Singapore. The two of them had walked the last two hours in the forest in complete darkness and came into the bar/restaurant a bit haggard and ready for drinks. Ivy quickly identified them as a source of information. She asked if they were going on the boat from Vilanova de Arousa as well. They confirmed but said that they didn't have any details regarding the boating situation. Juan Carlos and Ivy dove in on a plan. They eventually contacted a captain that agreed to take us as long as we had eight passengers. Planning our departure based on the optimal tides, the captain instructed us to meet him at the docks on Monday at noon. She assured the captain that we would have eight pilgrims and be ready to go. At that point, we were five pilgrims.

We were lucky to have Ivy in our pilgrim clan because for the next twenty-four hours, it was her drive and commitment to the plan that she manifested to reality. She approached nearly everybody we met and asked them of their plans from Vilanova. Eventually, she recruited another pilgrim from Brazil. Maria was seventy years old and had also walked from Porto, Portugal. She agreed to join our boat. Now we were six.

We met a very interesting Dutch pilgrim on the Camino—Simon— that also agreed to make the boat journey with us. Simon made seven. That night, we all met for dinner in the Vilanova to discuss our plan in the morning and for finding one more passenger. We made several toasts in the excitement of the pending boat ride and to the two remaining short days until our arrival at Santiago de Compostela. But we were still short one passenger. There was a Spanish pilgrim that Ivy pressed hard to join us as he walked through the restaurant, and he tentatively agreed to potentially meet us at the meeting place at noon the next day. He did not.

After a café con leche, some incredible pastries and a couple of shots of espresso, Ivy, Sergio, and I arrived at the docks about an hour ahead of schedule in hopes of confirming our last passenger. I walked down and visited with the captain as he prepared the boat. He asked, "Where is Ivy?"

I pointed to the office up above to where Ivy and Sergio were waiting for the rest of the group and Ivy was campaigning for one more passenger. In Spanish, the captain asked if I knew Ivy. I told him that we had met on the Camino. He said that he had a few dozen emails, voicemails, and texts from her, but he had no idea what she said because he did not speak English!

The Spiritual Variant Boat Crew Pilgrims from Singapore, Portugal, Brazil, Holland, Taiwan, Spain & United States

When the rest of our boat party arrived at the docks, we were still short one passenger. We had made a plan that if he refused to go with only seven, then we would just split that extra fare; and with that, he would surely agree to take us. I approached the captain and shared the news that we had only seven passengers. He smiled and said in Spanish, "Not a problem. If I do not take Ivy and her friends, I'm afraid she will continue to call and text me for the next few days. Anything to make it stop! Now get on the boat!"

He laughed, and the rest of our crew asked what he had said. I relayed to the pilgrims, "He agreed to take the Magnificent Seven at no extra price!"

We were off and on our way to Padron. The adventure of the Spiritual Variant, the angelic singing nuns of the monastery of Armenteira, Ivy's persistency, and our willingness to trust her in commandeering the captain of our incredible boat ride, left us with memories and friendships that we will all treasure and cherish for the rest of our lives.

Chapter

6

Peace and Love, Not Just for Hippies!

On my Camino walking from Santiago to Finisterre, between Olveiroa and Cee, the rain had mostly cleared for the day. I walked by myself on this beautiful day in and out of fog from the top of a small mountain pass down to the coastal town of Cee. I walked into an incredible valley with open green fields occupied by the Rubia Gallega, a breed of cattle that are seen throughout Galicia. Thick pine and hardwood forests lined the ridges and edges of the pastures. For those having experienced the Northern California and Oregon Coasts, you can visualize what my views were on this particular morning.

Coming down into the valley, there was a small ancient church sitting off by itself. It appeared to be in good condition, but had not been visited by parishioners in the recent past. Parked next to the chapel was a ready-made "rest stop." And when I say rest stop, I mean a small camp trailer manned by a group of hippies.

Peace & Love Camino Rest Stop

As I approached their trailer, one of them asked where I was from. I answered that I was from America, and they asked, "Where in America?"

"Idaho."

They all replied in unison, *"My Own Private Idaho!"* (Referring to the 1991 cult classic movie with River Phoenix and Keanu Reeves.)

We all laughed, and they asked if I was hungry or thirsty. They had a wide range of drinks, pastries, and fruit to choose from. Like many venders along the Camino, this was a *donativo*. What that typically means is that they don't have a business license or pay taxes, so they don't charge for their goods but, rather, suggest that you donate. I enjoyed a warm cup of coffee and a mango and left them with a few euros in their basket. I learned that one was from Italy, one from South America, and one from Madrid. We had a nice short visit about the Camino and of their experiences working the "rest stop" and how their real home and hangout was back in Finisterre.

The Italian hippie reached out and handed me a card. It was a business card for some kind of a place in Finisterre. The card read as follows: "THE WORLD FAMILY. A PILGRIM'S COMMUNITY." It was followed by an address, social media connections, and information on their vegetarian and vegan menus. They invited me to please stop in and see them in Finisterre.

I thanked them and told them that I would … while thinking to myself that it was highly unlikely. Off I marched solo up and out of the valley and onto the small coastal village of Cee.

Fast-forward to the day after Cee. My old nemesis the rain returned. A few miles out of Cee and all the way into Finisterre, I walked through what can only be described as a twelve-mile walk through backyard lawn sprinklers! This was to be my last day on the Camino. I was tired, cold, wet, and, to be honest, a bit grumpy. As I walked into Finisterre, I told myself, *No matter the bar or restaurant, the very first place I see, I am going in out of the rain, taking off my jacket and poncho, and going to order the biggest beer they have and just drink!*

Finisterre was especially quiet on this rainy afternoon. The streets seemed to be vacant of any villagers, pilgrims, or even cars on the road. I came into town and made the first left toward what seemed to be the town center. I kept a keen eye out for that "first bar" to stop and have that giant beer. Then I saw it. First, I wiped my eyes to make sure I was seeing it correctly. I refocused and looked again … There in front of me, the first bar that I came to was the World Family Bar!"

World Family Bar

I smiled and probably even laughed to myself as I made my way to the door. I walked in the door and pulled back my poncho off of my head, revealing my face. At which point, again all in unison, a resounding welcoming greeting: *"My Own Private Idaho!"*

I was back with my hippie family, laughing, and, at long last, dry with a giant beer to celebrate the end of my first Camino and the fact that I would not be walking in the rain for, at the very least, the next few hours until I found a place to stay and eventually made my way out to the actual point at Finisterre.

No matter how long you have known a friend, it is always a warm feeling to see friendly faces. My short time with Team Donativo in that small valley with their travel trailer food truck next to the old abandoned church was enough time to know that, once again, I was with my people, and the Camino provided!

Chapter

7

History: A Fun Loving Hermit and His Psychedelic Dream

Camino Primitivo Family, 2019

As mentioned in chapter 5, the headless body of St. James was brought back from the Holy Land via a stone boat, brought ashore in Padron and then carted twelve kilometers inland to a resting place known as Compostela. And there, on this hillside, under a field of stars, Santiago came to rest ... for the next eight hundred years!

After so many years, the story was forgotten. The location of the resting place for one of Jesus's twelve apostles was lost to time. So many generations had passed that other than the stories of St. James having come to the Iberian Peninsula in the first place, little more was known by the majority of the people. Then one day a loner named Pelayo was out in forest hanging out when he saw lights and a sky filled with shooting stars. I'm not sure what Pelayo was up to when this episode was going on, but he decided to take a nap. OK, I take that back, I have a pretty good idea of what ol' Pelayo may have been up to!

In the year 813, after seeing the light show on the hillside, Pelayo had a dream. He had a vision of the sky filled with shooting stars on a hill. In that dream, St. James came to him and showed him the place of his tomb on that very hilltop. While in a dream state, Pelayo went to the hill and discovered the long-forgotten and hidden tomb. He then woke up at a marbled mausoleum covered in vegetation. He managed to open the tomb to find the body of James the Greater.

Santiago's tomb in the Cathedral

Pelayo shared his findings with the local bishop, who in turn notified King Alfonso II in Oviedo. Upon hearing of the finding, King Alfonso II and an entourage set off from Oviedo to the tomb of Santiago to verify and behold the resting place of one of Jesus's apostles. With this trek, King Alfonso II became the first pilgrim, and this route is now known as El Primitivo. The name is not for the fact that it is necessarily primitive but, rather, the *first* or *original* Camino. Later in this book, I will share some of my stories and experiences on the Primitivo Route. It is one of my favorites and, perhaps, the most beautiful!

With the discovery of Santiago's tomb in Compostela in the ninth century, the Camino de Santiago became a reality! Soon after Alfonso's first pilgrimage, others followed. Christians from all parts of Europe began making the pilgrimage to Santiago. At that time, the main reason for making the pilgrimage was faith. Santiago de Compostela became the third major Christian pilgrimage after Jerusalem and Rome. Today pilgrims come not only from Europe, but from all over the world—even Eagle, Idaho!

Chapter

8

Are You Steve from Idaho?

Glowing Pilgrims, Camino Portuguese, 2020

Previously, I mentioned my Camino friend Juhwan and his magical flashlight saving me from my predicament in the rain and mud. I also talked about walking into the small fishing village of Cee. Interesting fact about Cee: it is Europe's only Atlantic rainforest, which I indeed experienced firsthand. In the heart of Cee is a plaza, a church, shops, restaurants featuring the famed Galician seafood. At the edge of the port is a sea wall with a walking path that surrounds the port and bay itself.

Upon my arrival, I checked in to my lodging for the night and hung my clothes up to dry. I took a warm shower and then headed out into the center of the village to find something to eat and do a little exploring. I walked out to the bayfront and onto the walkway that led around the bay. The tide was high, and I noticed that there were large schools of fish swimming up against the seawalls and into the deeper waters of the bay. Leaning up against the cement and rock wall was an elderly man. He was very typically Spanish. Wearing an olive-green sweater, white button-up long-sleeved shirt, brown pants, leather shoes, and the quintessential European flat cap (beret-type hat worn by old European dudes throughout!), he was everybody's Spanish grandpa.

I asked him in Spanish, "Excuse me, señor, but do you know if people catch and eat these fish that are everywhere in the bay?"

He replied in the gravelly voice of a man that had seemingly been smoking dark filter-less tobacco since Franco was still in charge, "No, nobody eats these fish. They are 'trash' fish, bottom feeders that only come up into the bay during high tide."

Well, I had my answer. I thanked el señor and continued my walk around the bay. A few minutes later, a Korean lady approached me and asked if I knew anything about the fish below and if they were edible. Since I had just recently become an expert on the local fish in the bay, I shared with her what I had learned.

I asked her where she was from, and she said South Korea, but that she lived and worked in Virginia. She asked where I was from, and I replied, "Idaho."

She paused and asked with great surprise, "Are you Steve from Idaho?"

I quickly had a million thoughts going through my head. Did I do something that people were warned about this crazy character from Idaho? Were there posters in albergues advising to stay clear of "Steve from Idaho?" After a few awkward moments, I sheepishly asked, "Why, what did you hear?"

She laughed and said that she knew Juhwan and had hiked with him that day and previously on other days. He had told her about me, my brother living in Seoul, and, unfortunately, even the hike in the dark without a flashlight!

This really wasn't a "seven degrees of Kevin Bacon" kind of a connection, but it was a small-world coincidence, for sure. I reached out via email with Juhwan back in 2018 after that first Camino, but I have not spoken with him since. I have often thought about him and hoped that his new job has worked out for the best. Or, selfishly, that it didn't work out at all and that someday, somewhere I would run into him again on a Camino somewhere along the Way! Either way, I wish him the best. And on another note, ever since our first encounter in the rain and dark, I always carry a headlamp in my backpack!

As one walks on the Camino, the Camino family continues to grow, and the connections become intertwined. Life is often similar in that sense. What brings us together far outweighs what makes us different. If we pay closer attention to those connections, it is much more likely to have the support you need when you need it most. The Camino encourages new relationships, and perhaps with people that we would not typically have the opportunity to bond with and befriend.

Chapter

9

The Original El Camino for Dummies Guidebook (The Codex Calixtinus)

In the Middle Ages, the Camino was a difficult and dangerous journey. Depending on their origin, it could take a year to walk to and from Santiago. Motivations for pilgrims doing the Camino were asking for forgiveness, fulfilling a vow, seeking religious answers, punishment by a judge, or penitence by a confessor for sins perpetrated by the pilgrim. I especially like that last part. I wish there was still that option for some lawbreakers today. A chance to either go to prison for a period of time or walk for a few months thinking about their crime/sin and how best to get their lives back on track and be a better person. Obviously, I wouldn't want to stay in an albergue with a bunch of murderers and rapists, but less violent offenders may benefit from a long walk! I for one would choose some Camino time over jail time for speeding tickets and back taxes!

Back in the Middle Ages, pilgrims traveled in groups in an attempt to protect themselves from thieves and the elements and a better chance of finding the actual path. In the early times, the trail was not as well marked like it is today. A wrong turn could lengthen your journey days, or even weeks. Today, many pilgrims set off solo on their pilgrimage and usually find their Camino family somewhere along the way. Although very safe today, those same concerns are alleviated by walking, talking, and learning from others you meet along the Way.

In the twelfth century, there was an event that forever changed the pilgrimage. Pope Callixtus II set out to assemble the top scholars of the day to create a guidebook intended to give pilgrims advice, descriptions of the route/s, information on local customs along the way, and information about St. James himself. The Codex Calixtinus includes sermons, reports of miracles, and writings specific to St. James. With the Codex, pilgrims were armed with the original *John Brierley Camino Guidebook*, and away they went!

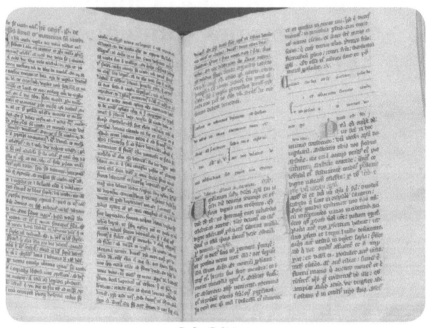

Codex Calixinus

One of the most interesting parts of the Codex is Book IV, "The History of Charlemagne." As you now know, it's the history of the magical appearance of St. James at the Battle of Clavijo. This chapter is about Charlemagne's time in Spain and his defeat at the Battle of Roncevaux Pass. This battle actually predates Clavijo, but the story tells of how St. James appeared in a dream to Charlemagne asking him to please "get me out of this tomb" and showed him the path to where his remains were hidden in the mausoleum guided by the Milky Way.

He obviously did not heed St. James's pleas for his discovery, but he did continue to appear to Charlemagne as he battled the Moors.

Along with Clavijo, this account of St. James appearing to Charlemagne while fighting the Moors was perhaps just more early propaganda by the Catholic Church to rally more to join military orders in the fight against the Moorish invaders. These same military orders that formed during the Middle Ages were the same that later headed to the Holy Lands to fight in the Crusades. In later years, St. James's "Matamoros" persona was softened from the warrior status that came eight hundred years after his death. It is interesting how he was used to rally in war when in life, he continued the lessons of peace and forgiveness. This ties in with my earlier thoughts about how religion too often takes a narrative that has nothing to do with religion itself.

Chapter

10

The Postcard That Launched
a Thousand Ships!

I grew up in a small town, Cottonwood, in Northern California. I am the oldest of three boys. My father was a rancher and the county constable/marshal. My mother was a nurse in the small doctor's office in our town. I first caught the travel bug as my family traveled a lot around the United States. But I want to be clear: In the 1970s, we did not fly to our destinations. We piled into cars or campers and drove... and drove ... and drove. If lucky, we camped; and if we were really lucky, we stayed at a Motel 6!

My first taste of Europe was in the summer after high school graduation with a group of recently graduated students from various high schools around the west. Over the course of two weeks, we flew, bussed, trained, and ferried through eight countries in Western Europe. Oddly, Spain, and Portugal were not on that itinerary. But with that trip, I was hooked and knew that I wanted to get back someday.

I attended Humboldt State University (now Cal Poly Humboldt) in Arcata, California, and I got a degree in geography and studied art in 1991. After college, I spent six months in Alaska working in a cannery in Kenai/Soldotna, operating a backhoe, and backpacking for a few months in the wilds of Alaska. I returned to Arcata in the late fall and went back to work for a local brewery in the bar/restaurant/concert venue as a manager, where I had worked while going to school. The brewery was owned by an ex-NFL player. You can look up his name, but let's call him Antonio...

In August of 1992, on my way into the brewery to work one morning, I checked the mailbox as I pulled out of the driveway. Along with a few bills and ads was a postcard from Spain. The postcard was from a college buddy, Chuck, who had gone to Spain on an exchange program and never really came home. The photo on the front of the postcard was of the Alhambra Palace in Granada, Spain. On the back of the postcard was written these words that changed my life's trajectory forever: "Dude, I live in a five-hundred-year-old house. Rent is cheap. Cocktails are cheap. Food is cheap. Women come and cook and clean for me. It's natural and correct ... when are you coming?"

The only other thing on the postcard was a phone number after the "When are you coming?" Chuck was (and still is) a bit of a character. Upon reading the postcard, I laughed to myself and stuffed it into my jacket pocket, and off to work I went.

I arrived at the brewery with Antonio waiting for me in the office. He was terribly upset over something that had happened with the books or deposit from the night before. I tried to explain to Antonio that the day before was my day off and I was not in at all. He wanted nothing to do with my explanation, or "excuses," as he put it. After taking the yelling and blame for all that was done wrong the night before, I said to Antonio, "Wait just a minute, I'll be right back!"

I walked downstairs from the office, reached into my pocket, took out the postcard, and, from the phone behind the bar, I dialed the phone number on the "Natural & Correct" postcard.

Ring, ring, ring ... "Hola."

"Is Chuck there?"

"Que?"

"Chuck, is there a Chuck at this number?"

"Eso que a la pagu los el osge un chico loco la, k, pore k?!" (At the time, I didn't speak Spanish, and I had no idea what he was saying, but the guy on the phone was yelling all kinds of words into the phone in Spanish.)

He then shouted, "CARLOS!"

A few moments later, I heard Chuck's voice come onto the phone and say, "Si, Digame ..."

The number on the postcard was that of Chuck's girlfriend's house, and the angry Spaniard was his girlfriend's father. I relayed to Chuck that I had received his postcard, and we both laughed. I then asked him, "Were you serious about asking me to join you in Spain?"

Chuck replied, "I just got a new apartment in the center of Granada, and I need roommates. Yes, I am serious."

I quickly answered, "I will be there in two weeks!"

I marched upstairs and announced to Antonio that I was out! And that is how and when my Spanish odyssey began.

As a twenty-three-year-old, the small fortune that I had amassed consisted of a jeep, a motorcycle, two large fish tanks, and a futon! In two weeks from the "Natural & Correct" postcard and phone call, I had sold all my possessions, dropped my dog with my folks, bought a one-way ticket to Madrid, and was off. Two days later, I was living in an apartment in the center of Granada with Chuck and later our third roommate, Roberto. The date was September 5, 1992.

Roberto was Canadian, but his parents were from a small town in Galicia—Mugardos. Roberto had been traveling around Spain on a motorcycle before settling in Granada to study language. I thought that I could get by with my two years of Spanish in high school. However, in short order, I realized that I was inept when it came to communicating with Spaniards. I was able to enroll at Lenguas Modernas, La Universidad Granada. A few weeks later, in an intensive four-hour-per-day Spanish language class.

Our apartment was on the fourth floor, no elevator. On our floor, there were two apartments. One with Roberto, Chuck, and myself. In the second apartment on the fourth floor lived four women students, three from Spain and one from Cuba. Two of the Spanish girls were sisters from Jerez de la Frontera, Cadiz. They were both studying law.

Since this is a story about St. James and El Camino de Santiago, I don't want to get too far into the weeds at this point about what I had for lunch in Granada during those days ... but I will say that my time in Granada left me with a passion for Spain. So much so that I married one of those Spanish sisters from Jerez de la Frontera. I met Maria Eugenia Espinosa Corbellini while living in that apartment on Puente del Carbon, Granada, and my life changed forever.

Chapter

11

My Camino Pledge

Glowing Pilgrims, 2020

While living in the apartment with Chuck and Roberto, I was able to travel and explore Spain. And on one particular getaway, I was lucky to head north with Roberto and a Swedish student we had befriended,

Mats. The three of us rented a car and drove up to Roberto's parents' hometown in Galicia, Mugardos. We ate the most incredible seafood and investigated beautiful fishing villages that lined the green hills and mountains up and down the north Spanish coast. During one of our days exploring, we stopped off in the city of Santiago. I knew nothing of the story of St. James or the famed Camino pilgrimage. I did see that it was a vibrant town with a lot of young people, bars, restaurant, *life*. With that, we spent the day walking the streets of Santiago, tasting all of the incredible dishes and drinks typical of this region.

Today, I can still remember the moment we walked out onto the Plaza del Obradoiro in front of the cathedral in Santiago for my first time. Even when one knows nothing of St. James or of the Camino itself, the very special and powerful feeling is unique and enters your core. That energy flows through the cobblestones, up over the cathedral's high bell towers and then back connecting all the people there in that moment with all of the past that have passed by this sight over the millennium.

Some say that this energy felt in Santiago and on The Camino itself is because The Camino runs along one of the earth's meridians, also called a ley line. Long before Santiago himself set foot on the Iberian Peninsula, pre-Roman pagans walked this same path being pulled by the same mystic allurement. The paths along the ley lines are said to be electromagnetic energy and to have healing qualities. The idea of ley lines was made even more popular in Shirley MacLaine's book, *El Camino*. She believes that several ley lines intersect along The Camino de Santiago and their energy brings clarity and thought. I'm not sure I agree with Shirley MacLaine on a lot, but I do buy into her advocacy of "there's something going on here!"

Additionally, it is believed that The Camino is perfectly parallel with the Milky Way. The name *Compostela* comes from the *Latin campus stellae*, "field of stars." Whether it be the Druids, the Celts, or, ultimately, the Christians, history has proven that the draw to this particular place on the planet for a very long time. The enigma of this spiritual juju crosses through time and space and whether one believes in this aspect of the Camino lore or not, the fact that into the twenty-first century people are still feeling the calling certainly makes the story that much more compelling.

Back to my inaugural walk out onto the plaza facing the cathedral. There were people sitting in small circles, some still wearing backpacks, others with backpacks on the ground. This was the spring of 1993. I don't believe the numbers of pilgrims were the same as a typical spring on the plaza today, but it was obvious something was going on. The pilgrims appeared haggard, dusty, weathered ... yet extremely happy, excited, singing, smiling, laughing, *glowing*!

I stopped and turned to Roberto and asked, "What the hell is going on here?"

Roberto answered, "They are pilgrims."

Having not a clue what he was talking about, I questioned, "Pilgrims? Like turkey eating pilgrims?"

He gave me the look that as an American, I was kind of used to getting from people that had traveled more than me and knew more "worldly" things than this kid from a small rural town in the sticks.

He smartly said, "They are pilgrims that just walked on El Camino de Santiago."

In that very moment, I said to myself that I was going to do this walk someday. I didn't know when. I didn't know how. But I knew that I had to come back to Santiago and learn how *to glow* like these pilgrims.

Chapter

12

Cheers to Women with Poor Taste!

Maria Eugenia's thing for a poor painting
vagabond with a bad accent

You'll have to read about all of my Andalusian adventures in my next book! To shorten this time into the CliffsNotes version, Maria Eugenia and I met in the fall of 1992. Over the Christmas holiday, my roommates were both leaving for the holidays, and I planned to stay in Granada, ski and paint. Side note: I have degrees in geography and art. While living in Spain, I painted and sold paintings to make extra money to extend my time and travel.

Knowing that I was going to be alone over the holidays, Maria Eugenia invited me and one of my Spanish language classmates, a Greek girl, to join her and her sister with their family in Jerez. Her brother drove up to Granada and picked us up, and we spent nearly a month with her family and friends in Jerez, El Puerto de Santa Maria, and Cadiz. It was at this point that Maria Eugenia and I started dating.

Eventually, the fish tank/jeep/motorcycle money ran low, and the painting sales weren't enough to feasibly extend my comfortable life in Granada. I headed back to Northern California in the summer of 1993. Having graduated from college, traveled to Alaska for six months, and now having just spent just short of a year in Spain, at the urging of my parents, I decided it was time to start thinking about a "real job." I enrolled in a teaching credentialing program at a small private college in Redding, California. Maria Eugenia did come out and spend a month with me over the next summer, and upon her return to Spain, I was unable to focus on anything else other than finding a way to get back to her and her wonderful country. Eventually, this uncontrollable draw had me back dropping off my dog at the folk's house and purchasing another one-way ticket to Madrid!

From 1994 through 1995, I lived with Maria's family in Jerez and El Puerto. Those years solidified my love for Maria Eugenia and her culture, language, cuisine, and perhaps even starting my passion for El Camino that I have today. We married in the US to start the immigration process on November 13, 1995, and then in the Cathedral de Jerez on April 13, 1996, along with thirty-four friends and family from the United States that made the journey over to join Maria Eugenia and her friends and family for a wonderful celebration between both cultures. Language was not an issue. My family gained a daughter and her family, an American with a bad accent and love of all things Spanish!

Steve & Maria's wedding at the Cathedral de Jerez la Frontera, April 13, 1996, with family

We moved back to the United States in 1996, living first in Northern California, then Oregon, and ultimately settling in Eagle, Idaho. We have lived in Eagle since 1998. We have two children, Danielle (Daniela) and Paul (Pablo). Maria Eugenia's family are all still in Spain, and we get back as much as possible to see them. Once the kids are grown and out of college, our plan is to split time between here and there.

After our wedding and before my first eventual Camino, I was lucky to make it back to Santiago on two different occasions, each concreting my need to return and learn all that I could about El Camino and Santiago. I even took my parents to Santiago and told them about El Camino and the fact that I was going to make the pilgrimage someday, they got it. As we can all attest, time can be cruel, marching faster and faster as we get older. I think generally, there are two kinds of people in life. Those that are always getting ready to do something and those that actually do it! I drew a line in the sand and made a promise to myself: I would be a pilgrim on El Camino de Santiago before my fiftieth birthday!

On the early morning of October 8, 2018, just four months shy of my fiftieth birthday, I was taking my first steps on El Camino de Santiago! I have since walked a total of four of the Caminos and hope to be walking them until I am physically unable. At which point, I may start on horseback!

Chapter

13

The One and Only Camino

Many people were first introduced to the Camino de Santiago after watching the 2010 Emilio Estevez and Martin Sheen movie, *The Way*. The movie was a great introduction to the Camino for those that were not familiar. It was a calling for many as inspiration to walk the Camino for themselves. The one misleading aspect of the movie is that it portrayed El Camino de Santiago as one trail from Saint-Jean-Pied-de-Port, France, to Santiago de Compostela. And because of this, there is a lot of confusion regarding the Camino.

The truth is that there are over fifty thousand miles of trails that lead from all over Europe to the cathedral in Santiago, which holds the tomb of the apostle James the Greater. The busiest and most famous Camino is the Camino Frances. Oftentimes, the French route is incorrectly assumed to be the Camino. This is not the case. Within Spain and Portugal alone, there are enough trails that would be difficult to accomplish in a lifetime. But dang it, I am certainly going to try!

Camino Routes

In medieval times, pilgrims set off for Santiago de Compostela from their own homes, towns and villages. Different Camino routes were born over the centuries as pilgrims traveled from all corners of Europe and beyond. Today, as a result, pilgrims have many different routes to choose from, each of them with their own heritage, history, culture, and traditions.

Pilgrims today can choose a route that best fits their own unique circumstances. Some routes are more rugged and require more fitness and training. Others may be less difficult terrain and easier for the casual hiker. Some paths follow the coast while others wind alongside rivers and streams. One of the most important aspects of electing the route that is best for you is time. How much time you have to allocate for your Camino may dictate which route is best for you. As an example, the Camino Frances takes most pilgrims thirty to thirty-five days to complete. Many pilgrims may find that an impossible and difficult hiatus from work and family. Therefore, some pilgrims may choose to do the Frances in sections as time allows.

Everything that I have been talking about is with regards to "walking" on the Camino. But there are other options. Many pilgrims choose to ride their bikes. Some of the routes may be slightly different for bikers versus hikers, but they both follow very closely, and both sets of pilgrims stay in the same accommodations. There is another subset of pilgrims that I find very interesting, those that make the journey via horseback. I have only seen pilgrims on horseback on the French Route, but I have heard of people making long Caminos riding horses. I once saw a guy in Pontevedra that used a donkey to carry his back. And my favorite is the story, perhaps a Camino urban legend, of the Frenchman that walked to Santiago with seven goats, three donkeys, and a dog as his accompanied Camino family!

As previously mentioned, there is no right or wrong way of doing your Camino. There is just doing what works best with the time you have available, the terrain that best suits your physical abilities, and the route that checks all the cultural and historical boxes that most interest you. Or, if you are like me, you can start to check off each of the different routes one year at a time! Whether you choose the Camino Frances or the Portuguese Central Route, both are amazing and unique. Whether you choose the Camino del Norte or the Portuguese Costal Route, both are on the coast, and yet very different. You may choose to continue your pilgrimage to Finisterre and Muxia after Santiago or turn north and head up Camino Ingles. All are amazing and full of adventure and mystery.

There is no right or wrong Camino, just the Camino that best fits you.

Camino Routes, The Central Portuguese Route

Chapter

14

The San Francisco Spa
& Retreat, Santiago

On my second Camino, I walked El Primitivo with my seventeen-year-old daughter, Danielle (Dani). She graduated from high school in Idaho on June 2, 2019. On June 5, we were in Oviedo taking our first steps onto the oldest of the Caminos. Dani had been to Spain many times visiting her mother's family. This was the first time that it was just the two of us. Truth be told, I was excited about doing this walk with her, and she was doing it as a way to make her old man happy. But upon our completion, the look on her face proved that this time was something that will always be special for us both. I can think of no better way of launching her into life than by starting it off with time on El Camino de Santiago.

Several days into El Primitivo, we were walking up this awfully long gradual hill. We were in a forested area with a shaded trail that was noticeably quiet and far from any roads or villages. Dani and I walked side by side, each in our own thoughts and just walking at a steady pace. As we made our way up the long hill, a pair of Spanish women were walking at a slightly faster pace than Dani and me. The two women were talking to each other in Spanish. One of them said to the other, "We should have got a coffee before we left the albergue."

The second pilgrim: "I wonder when the next place is where we can get a coffee?"

For those that know the Spanish culture will attest to the fact that Spaniards take their coffee profoundly seriously. They drink a very strong coffee with steamed milk called café con leche. The morning café con leche is as much a ritual as it is an addiction for the Spanish. So this conversation between these two early in the morning was certainly nothing out of the ordinary.

The first pilgrim: "When we pass these *guiris*, we can walk faster and get a coffee sooner."

In Spain, the word *guiri* is a derogatory name for foreigners. Not derogatory like a bad or dirty word—just something said referring to the typical-looking foreigners. Originally, it was used for the British; but today, Spaniards often refer to all touristy foreigners as guiris. Similar to the way the word *gringo* is used in Mexico for Americans.

I had read the description of that day's walk earlier that morning, and I knew there was a cafe in another kilometer or so up the trail. As they passed Dani and me, I said in Spanish, "There is a place with coffee in about fifteen minutes or so up the trail."

They both stopped in their tracks, and one of them asked me, "Where are you from?"

I smiled and replied, "Guirilandia!" (It's my made-up name of the land of guiris!)

When hearing my Spanish, the fact that I referenced them calling us guiris, they both nearly died of embarrassment. But when I laughed, they then joined me laughing, and we were all smiles. I assured them that I was indeed a guiri and okay with that nickname. We all laughed some more.

I learned Spanish in southern Spain, Andalusia. The Andalusian people have a unique accent that is very distinctive from that of Galicians. They noticed my accent being part guiri and part "Andalu." They asked where I learned Spanish, and I shared that I had studied in Granada and lived in Jerez for several years and that I was married to una "Jerezana."

They were both from Cadiz, which is very close to Jerez! We didn't know any of the same people, but we did share stories of our favorite hangouts in both Jerez and Cadiz. Laura and Bea became the first two members of our Camino family on the Primitivo.

Upon walking farther up over the hill and down the other side to our first stop together, we shared a coffee break at the place mentioned in the guidebook. We talked more about the Camino, where we were from, and we began to get to know each other. It was also good for Dani to have two women to hang out with other than just Dad!

Bea asked me where we were going to stay when we got to Santiago.

I replied that we had reservations at a place, but nothing special.

Bea quickly jumped in, "Well ... Laura and I have reservations at the San Francisco Spa and Retreat. We are going to get massages, spa treatments, manicures and pedicures, steam baths… blah, blah, blah…"

Bea & Laura excited about their "Spa Resort"

I told her that it sounded nice, and after walking the next 250-plus kilometers, the spa treatment would be incredible. Dani kind of hinted that we should look into staying at the San Francisco Spa & Retreat in Santiago as well. I pretended that I didn't pick up on her hints…

We had a nice dinner with the girls, and the next day, we had breakfast and walked again. Once back on the Camino, Bea asked, "What are you and Dani going to do in Santiago? In case you didn't know, Laura and I are staying at the San Francisco Spa and Retreat, and we are going to have massages, spa treatments, manis and pedis..."

I assured her that yes, I was aware of their plans.

On the third, fourth, fifth ... and each and every morning until we arrived in Santiago would start off with the same question ... or affirmation as to how much better their time in Santiago was going to be than at our albergue or one-star hotel, wherever it was!

Fast-forward to the day we walked into Santiago and out into the plaza in front of the cathedral. It was a beautiful day, and I was especially grateful and wore a huge smile experiencing Dani walking into the plaza with our group of new friends and having the greatest sense of accomplishment and happiness. Bea, Laura, Dani, and the other members of our Camino family that we had picked up along the way all sat together in our glowing glory—that same glow that had captivated me back in 1993.

We spent most of the early afternoon soaking in the emotions and realizing that the moment was now becoming sad, realizing that our walking adventure was over. Eventually, we decided to each make our way to our individual accommodations to get cleaned up and take a nap. Obviously, it was one last time for Bea and Laura to share that they were off to start on their "spa treatments, mani, pedi, massage... and on and on." We all agreed that we would meet at a specific restaurant at 9:00 p.m. for our final goodbye dinner. With the plan in place, we all went our separate ways until dinner. On this particular weekend, there was both a beer and music festival going on in Santiago. We had all made reservations because we had heard that rooms were going to be difficult to find if we waited until our arrival.

At 8:45 p.m., we all received a text in our WhatsApp group text chat group from Bea and Laura that said, "We are going to be late for dinner. Start without us. We'll explain when we get there."

Bea and Laura showed up at the restaurant at about nine thirty with their heads hung low. Bea said, "Laura, should I tell them or you?"

Laura said, "Go ahead..."

"Well, after we left you at the cathedral, we caught a cab to the San Francisco Spa. The cabbie laughed when we said spa, but we thought nothing of it. He dropped us off in front of a small, little run-down, rough-looking hotel far from the center of Santiago. We went into the lobby to check in. The man at the counter said that he was sorry but they had no rooms left. We told him that we had reservations for the San Francisco Spa for the next two nights in Santiago. The man said that this was the only San Francisco hotel in the Santiago area and furthermore, they were not a spa..."

"But we have reservations that we made two months ago!"

"Senorita, can I see your reservations?"

"Yes, here they are ... see, June 15 and 16."

"Senorita... your reservations are for the San Francisco Spa & Retreat in Santiago... *Chile*... not Spain!"

Bea and Laura had been looking for a place to stay from this point until 9:00 p.m. when they had finally found what may have been the last room available in the entire city ... and obviously, without their massage, mani, pedi, and steam baths!

Sometimes the life lessons learned on the Camino are of humility. But in this case, the pure humor in the lesson gave the rest of us enough ammunition to continue giving Laura and Bea a hard time years after our time on the Camino. We still have a group WhatsApp chat going from 2019. In my travels around the US, each and every time I see a sign, business, or hotel with the name "San Francisco" on it, I snap a photo and send it to the group chat with a question for Bea and Laura: "Is this your spa?"

Chapter

15

Señor, Can I see Your Credentials?

Before you take your first step on El Camino de Santiago, there is a clerical issue that needs to be initiated. In order to be a legitimate pilgrim, one must carry with them an official Credential, or Pilgrim Passport. Sounds complicated, but you can pick them up at most albergues, hotels, and churches on the route or at any pilgrim's office for a whopping two euros. Procuring your credential is one of the most important features of the Camino de Santiago. It's both your ticket to ride and ultimate memento from your Camino. The credential grants pilgrims access to albergues and allows pilgrims to complete the Compostela. The Compostela is the certificate you are awarded upon completion once you can prove that you walked a Camino by gathering stamps along your Camino route. Your credential and the stamps serve as the proof that you made the journey and validates your routes, days, and stops along the way.

Pilgrim Passports

The Pilgrim Passport is a rectangular booklet folded like an accordion that is roughly the size of your country's Passport that you used to travel to Spain. To validate your starting point, you typically go to the church in the city that you start your pilgrimage from and ask for a "stamp." The stamp is usually an ink-pad-pressed stamp that has the logo of a business/restaurant/albergue/hotel, the coat of arms of a town/village, or the symbol of a church on it. You are required to get at least one stamp per day, but it is really great to collect as many as you can as memories of your adventure and stops along your Way. If your Camino is walking the last one hundred kilometers or biking the last two hundred kilometers, then you are required to gather two stamps per day.

Once you reach Santiago, what do you do with your credential? One of the best souvenirs pilgrims bring home with them is a Compostela Certificate. It is a unique reflection of your Camino experience. No two passports are the same as they have each and every one of your stamps from your individual Camino. Upon your completion in Santiago, your certificate can be obtained from the Pilgrims Office in Santiago.

Celebrating earning our credentials
at the Pilgrim's office, Santiago

Ivy and her credentials

The certificate is an official church document that states your name in Latin, where you started and the date of your starting point and arrival into Santiago. The process has changed over the last few years and I think due to COVID, the current system is much better. After my first and second Caminos, we stood in line for *hours* at the Pilgrim's Office to secure our certificate. Today, when you arrive in Santiago, you go on to the official Santiago Pilgrim's website and schedule a time to obtain your certificate. After my last pilgrimage, it literally took less than ten minutes from the time I arrived until I was out of the office and drinking a well-deserved glass of wine!

The history of the pilgrim's credential dates back to the Middle Ages. Having the credential allowed pilgrims safe passage along the way. Protection for pilgrims on the Camino was provided by the Knights Templar. The Pilgrim's Credential allowed free passage through kingdoms and countries. With documentation, often churches made asylum, food, and hospitals available to pilgrims walking to Santiago.

The Knights Templar were important pieces in the early history of the growing popularity of the Camino during the Middle Ages. Knowing that crimes against pilgrims were considered crimes against the crown and the church, having these highly funded and armed knights as pilgrim protectors weighed heavily on potential highway thieves. The Knights Templar were hired swords of the Church that kept the Camino safe.

Most of us have somewhat of an understanding of the Knights Templar and the crusades because of the movies on the topic such as *The Da Vinci Code*, *Assassin's Creed*, *Knights Templar*, *Kingdom of Heaven*, and *The Crusaders*. The Russell Crowe version of the Robin Hood story is another one that gives a historical hint of what it meant to be a crusader during this point in the history of Christianity.

The Knights Templar were officially endorsed by the Roman Catholic Church. They became a favored charity throughout Christendom and grew in wealth and power. Ultimately, this wealth and power became too much for the Catholic Church and the crowned heads of Europe. By the end of the thirteenth century, the Templars had established a system of castles, churches, and banks throughout Western Europe. In the early morning hours of Friday, October 13, 1307, King Philip of France and the Pope at the time produced a wide range of made-up charges against the Templars, including heresy, devil worship, spitting at the cross, homosexuality, fraud, and financial corruption. As a precedent of the day, the astonishing amount of wealth that the Templars had amassed was all taken over by the kings and the church. And on that fateful day of Friday the thirteenth, the Templars were jailed, starved, and tortured. Given the horrific extremes and methods of torture, most of the Templars confessed to false charges; others were burned at the stake. So long before the Jason was running around Camp Crystal Lake terrorizing teenaged campers, the curse of Friday the thirteenth had already been a thing for the Knights Templar. The horror slasher films just made it a new thing!

Contrary to what we know from stories and movies, not all the Templars were highly trained knights. Many more were actually bankers and accountant types rather than their Templar brothers, the warriors. They became prominent in Christian finance and managed a great deal of the economic infrastructure throughout Christendom. They developed an innovative financial structure that is still used today.

The Templars really were responsible for creating the world's first multinational banking corporation.

A very somber sad fact is that the world continues to be in this same "crusade," fighting over which God is the righteous God—the same God that each religion believes that *their* God is predicated on peace and love. The sad irony in this fact is that after nearly 3,500 years since Moses led the Jews out of Egypt, over 2,000 years after Jesus was nailed up on the cross, 1,400 years after Muhammad had his revelations in the cave on Mount Hira, and over 700 years since the last Crusades to the Holy Lands, we are still in a power struggle over who has the correct God. Even more ironic is that after 3,500 years of conflict, these three religions have more similarities in common than differences in the notions of sacrifice, good works, hospitality, peace, justice, pilgrimage, an afterlife, and a loving God with all one's heart and soul.

El Camino de Santiago is a Christian pilgrimage at its base. But it is so much more than that. The Camino is a place where *humans* can come together as *people* ... not identified by class. Religion is up to the individual, and judgment is not up to pilgrims on the Camino. Pilgrims are committed to the belief that we can all be good, do good, and instill that goodness in others. As a world, we need more Caminos—places for people to come together under the premise of brotherly love and acceptance. One step at a time...

Chapter

16

Toad Skin, Mmm!

On one particular morning on El Camino Primitivo, Dani and I were joined by our Spanish pilgrim friends from Cadiz for breakfast in a small café first thing in the morning. One of my favorite aspects of the Camino is that the Spanish café con leche can be had everywhere. Each and every cup is consistently, deliciously and caffeinated as though it was given to us directly from St. James to ensure pilgrims were awake and aware. For Spaniards, taking "un café con leche" throughout the day is as religious as making the sign of the cross when somebody says that this is the year their favorite soccer/futból team will win it all!

Cafe con leche y pain au chocolat

We were served our coffee, melon slices, a few very thinly sliced pieces of jamon Iberico, a roll, a freshly squeezed glass of orange juice, and a traditional flaky pastry called pain au chocolat. As far as I'm concerned, there is no finer breakfast in the world. And that is not just hyperbole since this is a book about Spain and its culture. The flavors of these very different menu items come together to create an orchestra like melody that just writing about it in this instance has my stomach yearning for a Camino Spanish breakfast.

Camino breakfast

As already mentioned, the coffee is the anchor of the team. All starts and stops with the coffee. Secondly, the "pain au chocolat." Pain is not referring to the Camino provided blisters on your feet, but rather the French word for bread. In Spanish, bread translates to "pan." A pain au chocolat is a small croissant with a single square of dark chocolat baked inside of the roll and is the perfect blend of rich buttery croissant and bitter-sweet dark chocolate.

Next comes the heart of soul of Spanish delicacies, jamon Iberico. For those not familiar with jamon Serrano/Iberico, think of prosciutto and then replace that with a flavor ten times more incredible. Jamon serrano is so important and valuable to the Spaniards that most have an entire ham bone displayed in their kitchens mounted in a "jamon stand" with a special knife specially designed to slice off paper thin pieces of the astounding ham and served to guests as a snack/tapa with a glass of wine or local Spanish beer. Spaniards can tell you where the best jamon comes from, which type of pigs taste the best, what the best diet for these special pigs make the best jamon and even…that the color of the pig's legs will tell you how good it is going to be. Pata negra (black-hooved) pigs are considered the best tasting and most valuable. Pigs that roam the Spanish countryside feeding on acorns are also considered key to the best-tasting jamon. One of the most unusual aspects of a foreigner's first visit to Spain is that in most local bars and cafés, jamons are displayed hanging from the ceilings of the restaurant. Just hanging there above your head as you sit at the bar! Made from the best acorn-eating, black-hooved pigs raised in Andalucía, jamon iberico can cost up to $4,500! To be clear, I suspect that the jamon served to us at breakfast was not of the $4,500 variety, but still mouthwatering heaven!

Spain is also home to the orange tree. In many regions of Spain, the city streets are lined with orange trees. In Valencia, the rolling hills are lined with orange trees for as far as you can see. There are three types of oranges in Spain. The kind that grows on the trees that line the streets usually aren't much for eating. Then there are the delicious sweet oranges that are well-deserved treats to enjoy along the Camino. I especially like buying the local oranges to put into my backpack for the trail because they come in their own "wrapping" and are easy to pack! The third kind of orange is the one used for making orange juice. Most cafés have these very interesting machines that have a basket on top full of oranges that are fed into a juicing concoction that, when turned on, creates a flow of thick, sweet nectar of a deep-orange-colored juice that is served in a small glass. I have traveled all around the world and I can say without question that the freshly squeezed orange juice in Spain is second to none.

Toad Skin Melon

And this brings me to the last item on the breakfast menu—the Spanish breakfast melon. It has a thick green-striped outer rind and pale green to white inner flesh with a mild melon flavor. It tastes similar to a honeydew melon, but different. I have never seen this melon anywhere except in Spain. Because of the green-striped outer rind, they are called Piel de Sapo. This translates to "skin of a toad," and they do kind of look like that. I have never eaten a toad, but I suspect the melon tastes much better!

As we enjoyed our morning harmony of tastes, I mentioned to the Gaditanas (Spanish name for people from Cadiz) that we don't have Piel de Sapo melons in America. They couldn't believe that we did not eat these incredible Spanish staples for breakfast as they did. I shared that we do have honeydews and cantaloupes, but not the Piel de Sapos. We all agreed that it was sad that we aren't able to enjoy these wonderful melons back home.

After breakfast, we set off on the Camino. Not sure how, but at some point, Dani and I were separated from the Gaditanas and the rest of our Camino family. We managed to walk ahead of them and ended the day several miles ahead of them when we finally stopped for dinner and a place to stay for the night. During our walk that day, Dani and I walked through a village that had a hardware/farm/garden store. Out front of the shop on the sidewalk was a stand of garden seeds for fruits and vegetables. Dani and I both paused and looked at the seeds, then at each other. We both had the same thought: *Piel de sapo seeds!* And lo and behold! Right there on the stand was a packet of the magical seeds that would give us access to the melons back home in America! We were both happy to bring these seeds home, not only for our own selfish love of eating these fruits, but also as a gift to Maria Eugenia, as a way to be reminded of the tastes and culture of her heritage back in Spain. We bought a packet, stowed them in my backpack, smiled giant smiles of doing something great, and headed back on the trail.

Later that evening, when we arrived in the village where we were to stay for the night, we texted the rest of the crew and identified a place where we would meet for dinner. They agreed on a place and time and also that they had a surprise at dinner waiting for Dani and me!

Dani and I got cleaned up, washed our clothes, hung them up to dry, took a short nap, and then headed down to the agreed-upon restaurant to meet our friends for dinner. When we arrived, they were already seated out on the patio in front of the café with tapas and drinks in front of them. As we approached, Laura and Bea stood and handed Dani a small bag wrapped with a bow on the front. We both were quite surprised by this wonderful gesture. We sat down, and Dani opened the bag … it was a package of Piel de Sapo seeds! They had walked by the same gardening stand that we had and saw the seeds and thought of Dani and me!

The friends that we have walked with for minutes, hours, days, weeks, or months on El Camino de Santiago may come into our lives for only a short period of time, but their impact and generosity stay with us for a lifetime. Many of the pilgrims that became part of my Camino family remain friends, and we are in contact via social media, WhatsApp, and texts. The bond we share is forever, and I am so very grateful for each and every one of them … and … for the Piel de Sapo melons that now grow in our garden in Eagle, Idaho!

Chapter

17

Walk, Eat, Drink, Sleep, Repeat

We have discussed a bit of the history and some of my Camino experiences, but for those still not quite understanding what the day-to-day experience of being a pilgrim might really be like, let's dive into the daily details in the life of a pilgrim on El Camino de Santiago.

After obtaining your Credential, the next big question is, "Where do I sleep?" The nightly quest for a place to sleep can be a part of the adventure, and for some, potentially a stressful component of your supposedly "stress-free" pilgrimage. There are many different options for accommodations. For the sake of conversation and information, I am first going to line out the options. Then address the differing ideologies when it comes to "what is the correct traditional way" versus "what is your best way."

I've mentioned the word "albergue" several times prior to this section. I'm not sure of the root of this word, but for us English speakers, an albergue is simply a hostel for pilgrims. For most albergues, a Pilgrim Passport is required to stay. There are three types of albergues: private, municipal, and parochial. The one thing that they all have in common is that they are the cheapest options. Pricing ranges from a donation to what you are able to afford to, at the very most, twenty euros per night. Most have large bunk rooms with many rooms. In a post-pandemic Camino, the crowded bunk rooms were required to have much fewer beds per room than prior to COVID. Some do have private rooms, but usually, they are hard to find. Some have nice bathroom/shower facilities, others not so much... Some will provide sheets/blankets others do not. Some have access to washing machines and great areas to socialize, like a lounge area or a large kitchen. One of the best aspects of albergues is that it is a chance to cook meals and eat with other pilgrims. The social aspect of albergues can be one of the most enjoyable parts of your Camino. Most are run by volunteers. Some of the more interesting albergues may be old historical buildings. There are some incredible monasteries with gardens and beautiful chapels along many of the Camino routes.

The downside to albergues is that there can be a lot of people in a small space. If one person is snoring, we all hear each and every breath, snort, and gasp that person makes—*all night long.* If one person is gassy in their sleep, we all share in that experience as well. For those that make frequent late-night trips to the restroom, well, you get the point. Also, as discussed prior, many pilgrims leave very early hours before the sun comes up. If you are a light sleeper, having other pilgrims a few feet away rummaging through their backpacks at 4:00 a.m. may leave you exhausted from lack of sleep if this trend continues night after night.

Most albergues also have a curfew that is relatively early, usually 11:00 p.m., so you have to be inside by 11:00 p.m., or you risk the change of being locked out for the night. In the morning, checkout is usually around 9:00 a.m., and the earliest you can check in is after 1:00 or 2:00 p.m. Some albergues do take reservations, but not all. Because of this, there is often a race to villages, where it is known that sleeping options are limited and vacancies may be difficult to secure. One of the most challenging aspects of albergues during the high season on El Camino is the daily quest for a place to stay that lines up with the mileage that fits your daily pace.

Other sleeping options are small hotels, pensiones, and casa rurales. The upside is they offer private rooms and bathrooms. Many include breakfast and may even have dinner available for an additional fee. Some of the best meals I have experienced on El Camino have been at casa rurales. Sometimes the casa rurales are very old farmhouses that have been turned into a bed-and-breakfast type of establishment. The downside is that you may not make the same connections with other pilgrims that you would by staying in an albergue. However, I have met a lot of pilgrims over breakfast in one of these homes. The non-albergue options are all more expensive, but you have your own room.

Here is where the "purest" stamp their feet and say that to be a "real" pilgrim, you have to stay in a room with twenty-four other pilgrims, sleep on squeaking old bunk beds, and wait in line for a toilet. Without these difficulties and experiences, you aren't really a true pilgrim. Personally, I think this is hogwash. If they were really the "purest," they would be walking in leather sandals, wearing burlap clothes, and drinking out of creeks and mud puddles. So when I see a pilgrim dressed like a pilgrim from the Middle Ages, then yes, he/she may have a point. I understand and appreciate the amazing camaraderie and tradition of albergues, but I don't think it is for everybody.

On my last Camino, I walked with a pilgrim from Singapore. He was dedicated to the pilgrim way of life in the idyllic purest form. He believed a "true" pilgrim walked with the absolute minimum of materials as far as the contents in the backpack, staying in the cheapest and barest of albergues and not enjoying the finest meals/wines when the opportunity presented itself. I admire and respect his commitment to what he believed to be the "right" way.

However, I disagree with him that his way is the "right" way and certainly not the only way. Each of us are on our own path. As an example, I have backpacked all over the Sierra Nevada mountains of both California and Granada, Spain. I have backpacked in the Rocky Mountains in Idaho and the Cascades in Northern California and Oregon. For most of those trips, I carried my food, clothes, tent, and sleeping bag; slept on the ground; carried cooking equipment; and, in some places, even a weapon for protection. For me, the Camino isn't a place to prove that I can be a minimalist and suffer for suffering's sake. It is about the experience of walking in the footsteps of the millions of pilgrims that have walked these paths before me. It is about having meaningful conversations with people from all over the world and learning to view the world via their perception. It is about learning more about me and how I can be a better me. My way is not the only way, nor is his way the wrong way. When we understand and accept that it is your Camino and your way, then your own acceptance and doors of perception will open.

I have stayed in albergues, small hotels, pensiones, and casa rurales. For me, sometimes I want to just plop down on my own bed, in my own room, take off all my stinky hiking clothes, and lie there not worrying about people coming and going or being quiet if I have to get up and use the restroom at 3:00 a.m. in the dark. Other times, when walking with a group of friends, it is great to find an albergue in which you can get a smaller room and all can be there together and enjoy an incredible conversation. In writing this, I had a couple of flashbacks to albergue lounges in which pilgrims had a guitar, and we sang songs together, drank wine, and laughed until our sore legs and blisters were all but forgotten!

I once had a conversation with an elderly British pilgrim lady in a casa rural over a very nice breakfast that was included. She asked where I had stayed the night prior. I told her the name of the albergue where I had stayed, and she replied, "Aww, albergues ... Albergues smell of pain and regret!"

Not sure that I 100 percent agree with her, but her statement is one of those moments that I have never forgotten, and I smile every time I think of her saying it!

So you have your Pilgrim Passport and slept in your first night's albergue. Now what? Well, you wake up, pack up your belongings, and head out of the door and into your first day as a real pilgrim. I like to fill the tank first thing in the morning with a cup of café con leche, a glass of the most incredible freshly squeezed Spanish orange juice, a piece of local fresh fruit, and at least one very European style rich pastry (see prior chapter for more breakfast details and descriptions). Sometimes I am able to enjoy such a breakfast immediately upon leaving the albergue, or if I was lucky enough to stay in a casa rural, breakfast may have been served as part of the accommodation price. Then the walking starts.

One of the most important aspects of the Camino is that *it is your Camino*. Some pilgrims walk fast and others quite slowly. It is not a race, nor is there a penalty for arriving late. They aren't awarding trophies to the fastest walking pilgrim. Although on a few of my Caminos, after perhaps drinking a bit too much wine after a long day, I may have qualified for the "Pilgrim Wino of the Day," to date, my ribbon and trophy on that front have still not arrived...

Walk until you're tired. Stop and take a break. Rest on a rock next to a stream, on a bench, or lie down in a field and watch the clouds drift by overhead. Sit in a village square and watch the locals wander through doing what they do throughout the day. Watch the flowers wave in the breeze and follow the leaves floating down the stream that have blown from the canopied forest above. Take the time to think about what you are doing and why. Ask yourself, *How can I be a better parent, a better spouse, a better person. What will I do differently when I return back home?*

Take this time to think about the important things in life. Back home, we are busy being busy and often neglect the actual "living" part of life. Take the time to greet every cow, smell every flower, and light candles in every church. Disconnect from your phone and connect with what is really important. *Who am I, what am I about, and where am I going?* The Camino can help you find your purpose. You can find tolerance (although you still may be tempted to smother that guy snoring in the bunk next to you with a pillow!). Energy grows through connection. The Camino allows one to both connect with others and disconnect from the distractions. The routine of walking on the Camino will change your perspective and allow you to see beauty in ordinary things.

Dan Mullins, Australian musician and famed podcaster of "My Camino: The Podcast," had a guest on his podcast that said something that I found so revealing in reference to the Camino: "Love and celebrate the ugly parts! Everybody smells, gets dusty, and are wearing the same clothes every day!"

This quote demonstrates the beauty in the fact that we are all really the same. The Camino helps peel away the pretense. Pilgrims are able to glow knowing that they are, at that very moment, the best versions of themselves. Now the challenge is to take that feeling back with you upon your return to everyday life.

Back to the daily Camino grind ... After getting out on the Camino and taking breaks to enjoy the surroundings, duck into a café for a quick bite to eat, rehydrate, or, if the timing is right, a glass/glasses of some of the yummiest local wines and beers that always taste way better on the Camino than anywhere else in the world! Then get back on the trail and walk some more.

Sometimes, around 9:30 a.m. or 10:00 a.m., many pilgrims like to stop in a café along the trail and get what has been dubbed "the Camino Second Breakfast!" This is a chance to enjoy another café con leche, piece of fruit, or rich pastry. One thing for sure is that if you go hungry on the Camino, it is your own damn fault!

One of my secrets to keeping the feet healthy is to change my socks two or three times a day. Keeping the feet dry is key to blister control. My strategy doesn't work 100 percent of the time, but I think I have had relatively few feet problems compared to others, and I stand by my dry feet stance. Also, I bring two pairs of shoes and depending on the trail that day, I switch them accordingly. I bring a pair of light hiking waterproof shoes and a second pair of trail runners that are better for the days that you are on pavement, cement, and cobblestone streets.

Going back to my spreadsheeting-pilgrim tendencies, if I haven't already booked ahead, I like to look ahead at options for the next night's target sleeping options and dinner. There are a lot of guidebooks that offer information on nearly every sleeping option along your Camino. Most of those have the address, and maybe even a phone number or email address, with which you may be able to make reservations. Depending on what time of year and which route you are on at the time dictates whether or not you'll really need to worry about reservations. I favor walking in late fall, long after the crowds and rush to beds are not as much of a worry.

Once you have arrive and secured your lodging, your "working" part of the day is not over. The best thing to do is to get your gear in order for the next day before you get rested so much that you fall asleep and don't take care of these last few very important pilgrim duties. I always immediately take a shower. A trick I learned from one of my favorite pilgrims, Dr. Gigi Tree, is to get your clean clothes ready and take into the bathroom/shower room with you. Then get into the shower wearing your dirty clothes! With some soap, wash them right there in the shower, wring them out, put on your dry clothes and then hang up your wet clothes to dry so that by morning, they are dry and ready to go into your bag for your next day's outfit! Side note: when you are packing for your next Camino, bring a small lightweight piece of twine to use as clothesline. Some rooms have hangers and places to hang clothes, others do not. My clotheslines have saved me many times and ensured my clothes were dry by morning!

The simplicity of the Camino makes us want more of getting by with less. One of my most valuable Camino lessons has been the realization that I don't need so much "stuff."

Chapter

18

El Menu Del Día y El Menu Peregrino

The cornerstones of both the Spanish and Portuguese culture are the flavors associated with their incredible local dishes. Since the Camino itself crosses through several different regions, the local specialties are unique and specific to each country, region, province, and often all the way down to a small village. Tasting the local traditional meals make the Camino adventure that much more special. Many of the ingredients are grown in the gardens and raised in the fields out behind the albergue, hotel, or restaurant where you are staying.

Menu del Peregrino

All along the Camino, you will find restaurants that have posted out front a sign that states, "El Menu Del Dia" or "Menu del Peregrino." Most restaurants have a daily special that is typically made up of bread, a bottle of wine or water, an appetizer, soup or salad, a main entrée, a dessert, and coffee. You can always order off of the regular meal as well, but usually, the daily specials are priced less expensive. And when I say "less expensive," I mean that eating in Spain and Portugal is very affordable. The menu del dia usually ranges in price from about eight and fifteen Euros. I am a huge fan of the Pilgrim's Menu because it is usually something typical of the area and made by the people in the kitchen that probably have lived in that city, town, or village their whole lives. The dishes served along the Camino have most likely varied very little over time. Eating local is another way to connect with the culture and history of the Camino.

Menu del Dia

As I shared previously, I lived in Spain for several years, and I am married to a Spaniard. So my love of Spanish food may be a bit of the heavy-handed variety because we eat Spanish dishes daily at home and my wife is a very good cook. She has a large garden, and per the Piel del Sapo story in an earlier chapter, she grows Spanish melons and pimientos de Padron in Idaho. So I want to admit that my next description of my favorite Camino foods may be heavy on the personal perspective. With that said, I know that some pilgrims that are vegetarians or vegans are able to find many delicious options along the way. But beware that if you are a very strict vegan, the Spanish are often not dedicated to "100%" vegan when things might be listed or labeled as so. Pork, eggs, cured meats, sausages, beef, and chicken are very important aspects of Spanish/Portuguese cuisine. Equally as significant is fish to the Iberian diet. Mostly seafood, but in some regions, trout can also be found on menus.

Fruit & Vegetable Market

If you really want to experience the local foods, you will be rewarded with a newfound respect of the Old World at its best by vising a local market. I am not referring to the "supermarkets" but the actual open markets. In the larger towns, the market will be indoors and consist of rows and rows of booths with local vendors selling their goods. The stands are usually divided up into sections of vendors that each sell fresh fruit, dried nuts, spices, vegetables, fish, meat, or bread. Just writing this paragraph fills my nose with the incredible smells that are like nowhere else. In most homes, the fresh ingredients are bought daily for the big late-afternoon meal that is eaten with the family coming home during the afternoon siesta.

Pulpo a la Gallega (Octopus)

For those that have not visited the Iberian Peninsula, you may be surprised by the fact that they eat a lot of french fries. Living in Idaho, you'd think that the potato thing would be a reminder of home... but I really don't eat fries that often. Don't be afraid to ask for vegetables, or even plain boiled potatoes instead. A typical side dish that is an alternative to french fries is boiled potatoes with green beans topped with olive oil and a bit of wine vinegar. Another thing that pilgrims may not have experienced before is pulpo. Pulpo, octopus, is a dish that is very famous in Galicia. It's usually boiled, cut into small pieces, served on a small round wooden plate topped with olive oil and paprika and with fresh bread. Although some people won't go near pulpo, it is one of my absolute favorite tastes of Spain and with each and every pilgrimage that I've made, when I walk into pulpo country, I order it at every chance I get!

Fish Market

Fish is a very important staple in Spanish and Portuguese food. An interesting fact about Madrid is that even though it is far from a coast, the city of Madrid is considered one of the best cities in the world for seafood lovers. Seafood is flown in daily to the landlocked city from the coastal regions of Asturias, Andalusia, and Galicia. With many of the most popular routes on the Camino relatively close to the coast, the seafood found on the Camino is also very fresh. Mariscos (shellfish), bacalao (cod), calamares (calamari/squid), and gambas (shrimp) are found on many menu del dias along the Camino.

In an earlier chapter, I told the story of the "toad-skin" melons. I neglected to share that in addition to the seeds Dani and I purchased on that Camino, we also bought seeds for the iconic Galician pepper, the pimientos de Padron. One of my favorite dishes in Spain are fried pimientos de Padron and served with coarse sea salt. The peppers are sweet and mild, but famously, occasionally one of the peppers will be extremely spicy hot! And now that you are a pilgrim and know the story of the transfer of St. James's body from the stone boat to the altar to the cart and up the road to Compostela, you know that the body transfer occurred in the small coastal/river city of Padron, the namesake and original home to these peppers.

On the Camino, you will undoubtedly find Pilgrim's Meals that offer paella. My next comment is perhaps coming from a place of hearing my wife say this for the past 30 years. Paella is from the Spanish region around Valencia. You can order paella all over Spain…but it is never as good as the paella from Valencia. Because the restaurants along the Camino know that they are catering to foreigners, they will often times offer a paella as the menu del dia option. I am certainly not discouraging you from trying this option that actually might be very good; but know that it is ALWAYS better in Valencia! Now that I've got that public proclamation out of the way (making my wife and all Spaniards content on that paella public service announcement very happy), we can talk in more detail about paella!

Traditional paella comes in two varieties: paella Valenciana, which is made with rabbit and chicken, and seafood paella, which is made with… well, seafood! The rich golden-yellow color of the rice comes from saffron. Saffron a spice that comes from the pungent stigmas (pollen-bearing structures) of the autumn crocus flower. The spice is very expensive and not popularly known; in lower-level restaurants, they will actually use a yellow colorant instead of the flavorful saffron spice. Because only three stigmas are handpicked from each flower, it is considered one of the most expensive spices in the world. As an example, a pound of saffron represents 75,000 blossoms!

Tortilla Espanola, Menu del Dia

Another traditional Spanish staple is the tortilla Española. When I first arrived in Spain back in 1992, I incorrectly assumed that the food was going to be similar to the Mexican food that I had grown accustomed to living in California. Well, let's just say that I could not have been more wrong! Ordering a "tortilla" in Spain was my first lesson in the differences in Spanish and Mexican cuisine.

The history of the Spanish omelette, tortilla de patata, is believed to have started back during a war in the early nineteenth century when a poor Navarre housewife scrambled together a dish for a general upon a surprise visit. All she had was potatoes and onion and eggs ... and from that, the great tortilla Española was born. The tortilla Española is basically a potato omelette that is cooked in a nine-inch round skillet pan, flipped over when cooked, cut into pie-like pieces. A Spanish tortilla is at its best when the middle is still a little less than fully cooked

87

so that it is moist and not too dry. It can be served all by itself like a slice of pie or on a roll and as a sandwich. Tortilla Españolas are great to bring along on your Camino if you find a place that has it to go. Very typical to get a tortilla with a roll wrapped in aluminum foil to eat later.

We have all heard about the amazing ice cream from Italy, gelato. Well, I'm here to report that the Spanish ice cream is equally as amazing, rich and so dang amazing. I know I may upset my Italian friends by saying this, but perhaps, the Spanish helado is even better than its Italian counterpart! Helado is super rich, creamy, and full of unique flavors that are so incredibly profound that leaving Spain without eating ice cream should be a crime.

Whether you order the pilgrim's meal, the menu del dia, or right off the menu, the Spanish fare is worth jumping in all the way. Part of the cultural immersion is trying new things and experiencing what others think of as normal. Just as flamenco guitars, siestas, and Antonio Banderas are part of the Spanish identity, so is its food. Spain's approach to eating comes out in times of extreme wealth and great poverty. Through the ages, Spain has been at the top of the world and struggled greatly in poverty and hunger. The Spanish are a very proud people, and through the historical ups and downs, eating and sharing what they have is one of the most graciously beautiful aspect of the Spanish. Even when they have very little, they will share a meal. And perhaps even more than just sharing a meal, they will prepare something that would feed twice as many people that are at the table. Friends and family coming together to break bread is part of the Spanish fabric that is missing today in the United States. Sitting down and visiting, talking, eating, drinking, being together happens every day for Spanish families. Even when dining in restaurants, it is not uncommon for a group to be there for three hours. As an American, I am embarrassed to say how many meals I have eaten in my car while driving...

Café con leche

Juan Carlos, lamb shank & patatas

Spanish dinner in seaside town of Arcade

Croquetas

Chapter

19

Don't Even Think of Sitting with Me!

On my Portuguese Camino on the Central Route, I was walking with my Camino family, and we stopped into a restaurant that had a nice pilgrim's meal on the menu. The five of us walked into the small restaurant, and as we were looking for a table that would adequately accommodate us, Edyta stopped and announced to the group, "None of you better sit with me!" (When you are reading her statement in your head, do it in a Polish accent!)

Edyta

She walked past us and sat by herself in one of the smaller tables in the corner. Her husband, Antonio, just shook his head and sat at the table with the rest of us. Evelyn, Sebastian, and I had no idea what was going on. We assumed that Antonio was in trouble or she was upset at something that somebody in the group had said. The waiter first stopped by Edyta's table and took her order. He then came by our table and took our order.

He disappeared into the kitchen and returned with a glass of water for each of us and at our table. He brought a bottle of red wine, four glasses, and a basket of bread. He then returned to the kitchen and then back to Edyta's table with a glass of water, a bottle of red wine, one glass, and a basket of bread. Upon receiving her very own bottle of wine and a single glass, she picked up her backpack, bottle of wine, her wineglass, and basket of bread and joined us at our table!

Edyta became a student of the pilgrim's meal game. When you are with a group, they bring one bottle of wine for the table. If you are by yourself, they still bring one bottle of wine. Edyta proved the old Rolling Stones song to be spot on once again. You can't always get what you want, but if you try, sometimes you get what you need. And Edyta both wanted and needed her wine!

Let me shed a little light on my "Edyta needed her wine" comment. Edyta and Antonio are the most astonishing couple. Edyta is Polish, and Antonio, Portuguese. They both live and met in Saudi Arabia and have lived there for many years. Antonio is a music teacher at a school for expats, and Edyta, a nurse. For me, one of the most enjoyable aspects of the Camino are the pilgrims. You are given the opportunity to meet people from all over the world and learn about their culture and perhaps perspective regarding your own life. In the case of Edyta and Antonio, spending time with a Portuguese-Polish couple was rewarding in and of itself, but adding in the Saudi Arabia aspect made them a super dose of international intrigue. One of the many interesting stories that Edyta told was that in Saudi Arabia, alcohol was very strictly forbidden. They lived on a compound with a wall around their area inhabited by all non-Saudi foreigners there living and working. Inside of that compound, they would often have parties, and at those parties, people would have to make their own homemade wine, gin, whatever they could make.

Edyta said that when there was going to be a party, it was interesting to see all the people at the grocery store buying up all the juice and sugar. She said that she made a wine the last time that was terrible, but strong. She said that you could tell which was the good homemade hooch because it was drunk first. But eventually, even her bad-tasting homemade wine was all drunk! The things we take for granted!

Chapter

20

Camino Magic

Before setting out with my daughter Dani on El Primitivo, I shared with her that incredible things happen on El Camino that happen like nowhere else. I told her that we would meet fascinating people from all over the world, and that these experiences would stay with us forever. Attempting to "enlighten" a teenager on such things is nearly impossible if being sold by her "old" parent. If it would have been stated in a social media outlet, then perhaps she would have at least pretended to be more interested.

As we made our way out of Oviedo, I insisted that "something" special would happen soon. I promised her to just hold tight, and she would "feel the magic!" Well, we walked and we walked and we walked ... void of any "electrical mysterious energy," but as luck would have it, we had plenty of violent wind and sideways rain to question one's faith in anything!

At one point, we had a 2,500-foot elevation gain climb up and over a rocky pass called Puerto del Palo. We were cold and tired when we met Jose. Jose was walking with a friend over the pass and at one outcropping, they asked for us to take their photos and vice a versa with Dani and me. Jose said that he and his wife, Andrea, just moved to Galicia from Jerez. I asked if he knew my wife or any of her family, and he did not. From that point, we continued up toward the top of the pass. Perched at the top of the mountain was a small half-tube-shaped building with a door on one end and a chimney on the other. These buildings are typical in the mountains of Spain on and off of the Camino. They are called "refugios," or refuges from the weather.

Juan, his hiking friend & Dani on our way up Puerto del Palo, Camino Primitivo

Our "refuge" from the elements, el refugio

As the four of us walked toward el refugio, Jose asked me, "Would you like a cup of coffee?"

I replied, "Jose, you walked all the way up this mountain with coffee in your backpack?"

"No, silly, there is a road next to the pass and my wife is meeting us there with a thermos of coffee!"

We both laughed and made our way up the last few minutes up and into el refugio. Andrea arrived minutes later, and, as promised, she had a thermos full of coffee and a bottle of some kind of liqueur that was a welcome addition to our cold bodies. Andrea was about as tall as she was wide and was certainly a great host, pulling out cups for each of us, pouring our coffees, adding liqueur, and then serving it with the eagerness to ease our current tired states and warm our freezing cores. Andrea was just wonderful.

Andrea with Café & Liqueur

She told us about her new home and life in Galicia and how much they both loved the change of scenery from the south. Upon asking her about Maria and her family in Jerez, I learned that they actually attended the same high school. Andrea was about ten years younger, so she did not know her. As we sat in the small brick-and-cement hut, finally out of the wind and rain, she began to tell a story.

Andrea asked if I had ever heard of "manitas de Mocho."

I told her that I had not. She began to tell us the story of Mocho and his magical connection with El Camino de Santiago. Mocho worked in a toy factory in Alicante. He first walked the Camino in the early 1990s. He was so taken with his experience that he returned to walk it as often as he could. On his second Camino, he brought with him small plastic yellow toy hands that he had made as a hobby to give to children he met along the Camino. Later he gave them to pilgrims he met that helped him on his journey. He gave them to people that exuded kindness and Camino virtue. Soon people that had received one of Mocho's little yellow hands began telling others about this wonderful man that gave them their gifted "manitas." In Spanish, *mano* means "hand" and *manitas* means "little hand." *Manitas de Mocho* means "the little hands from Mocho."

Receiving my Manita de Mocho

If one had the good fortune of receiving one along the Camino, it was quite an honor. Pilgrims began asking where they could get a manita for themselves or to give to others. Mocho made it clear that his manitas could not be bought or sold, only given to somebody that made an impact on the giver of the gift. They are distributed via a handshake and without the recipient knowing that it is being given to them until they feel Mocho's little yellow hand in their palm.

Soon pilgrims began asking Mocho if they could buy the symbolic yellow hand. He declined to sell. Instead, he made them available to people if they donated money to charities, particularly charities that benefit children or cancer. In the beginning, there was one man, and one many only, handing out the famed Manitas de Mocho, but as time went on, there were more and more people that knew of the legend and the meaning of the little yellow hands, and they carried on the tradition up and down the Camino.

As Andrea and I stood next to each other, with our coffee and liqueur in hand and with Jose, his friend and Dani sitting on the bench in a small refugio, continuing in Spanish, asked Dani and me, "Did you understand the story?"

I gave her a nod in acknowledgment that I had. She paused, reached out to take my hand. Immediately, I felt the little yellow hand in my hand! Wow! I was so overcome with emotion. At last, we had our magical moment on our Camino de Santiago! I once read that goose bumps were God saying, "Pay attention!"

I had goose bumps and still get them when I tell, or even think about, this story today. I feel so blessed to have met Jose and Andrea and to have had this experience with Dani!

Even though there are hundreds of thousands of pilgrims that walk the different routes of El Camino each year, there is somewhat of a seemingly small community of famed pilgrims that gain notoriety through their guidebooks, movies, blogs, YouTube and Facebook pages and my favorite, podcasts. There are a lot of different formats and personalities that with a little bit of research, you'll find your own Camino guru to guide you on all that there is to know before and after you even step foot on The Way.

I have been fortunate to befriend several of these "friends of the Camino" and turn to them with my questions and look to their experience for sage advice. One such person is a wonderful podcaster named Guilherme Ribeiro from Braga, Portugal. Guilherme hosts a very popular podcast called *Camino de Santiago Pilgrim's Podcast.*

Guilherme knows more about the Camino, St. James, and the history than anybody that I've met. In fact, last year he was nominated and selected to be a member of the Universal Archconfraternity of the Apostle Santiago. This group was started in a 1499 mandate from Pope Alexander VI of faithful, clergy, consecrated, and laity, men, and women who work together to promote the apostle Santiago, the pilgrimage to his tomb and to the spread of his devotion throughout the world. At twenty-eight years old, Guilherme has done more to promote El Camino de Santiago than anybody could hope to do in an entire lifetime.

At one point, I was lucky to be one of the pilgrims that Guilherme interviewed on his podcast. It was an honor, and I enjoyed visiting with Guilherme and getting to know him, even if it was only virtually at the time. A year later, I arranged to meet Guilherme while I was walking the El Portuguese Central Route. We had a wonderful conversation about the history of the Portuguese route/s and a tour of the wonderful historical town of Barcelos. After a coffee and history lesson, we hopped into Guilherme's car and drove over to his hometown of Braga. I knew very little about Braga and was surprised by the hustle and bustle of the city center, an incredible vibe of commerce and movement. Just outside of the city, we meandered up a curvy two-lane road that winded up the mountain that overlooked Braga below. Sitting on top of the highest point was one of the most incredible landmarks that I've seen in all of Portugal, Bom Jesus do Monte.

The Stairs at Bon Jesus, Braga, Portugal

Bon Jesus, Braga, Portugal

Bom Jesus do Monte is a spectacular UNESCO-listed sanctuary that is situated directly above Braga below. Dating back to 1373, various chapels and churches have existed on this hilltop, with the current structure having been built in 1722. The famous staircase was listed by *Arch Digest* as one of the twenty top spectacular staircases in the world. My detour with Guilherme was truly an unexpected gem of an experience. Usually, the best things that happen on the Camino and in life happen when you least expect it.

After our visit to Braga and up the mountain to Bom Jesus do Monte, we drove back to Barcelos and to the Camino route where I would continue my Camino from where I had stopped earlier that day. Before leaving Guilherme, we sat in a café in Barcelos and discussed my days ahead on the Portuguese route and what to expect. As we finished our coffees, Guilherme asked me if I had heard of the story of Mocho and of his Manitas de Mocho. I smiled a giant smile and instantly returned to the moment in that small dark refugio with Andrea, Jose, and my daughter Dani. Guilherme reached into his pocket and reached out to shake my hand … and I instantly knew that I was receiving my second priceless sign of friendship and the greatest gift of El Camino de Santiago!

Guilherme with Manitas de Mocho

Several days after my incredible visit with Guilherme, I met one of my favorite peregrinas that I had met on any of my walks. Evelyn was quiet, soft spoken, but quick witted and quite hilarious if you paid attention. Her charm came in subtle looks and her summation of things said in a few words with spot-on accuracy that made you pay close attention to what was being said. I would say that she was a great listener, but perhaps that is only because I tend to talk way too much, and she didn't have the opportunity to get in a word!

Evelyn

Evelyn is from Mexico City. She had been living and working in Dublin for the last four years. She said that she moved to Dublin to become proficient in English. Upon hearing this, I asked her, "You moved to Ireland to improve your English?"

Evelyn replied, "I now know that was not best place to go to learn English!"

We walked together for about eight days and picked up more pilgrims along the way that joined our Camino family over those last eight days. Eventually, our group of five pilgrims shared a few final days in Santiago, and then with three of us heading out to Finisterre. On the second day of walking with Evelyn, we each had reservations for places that were about a mile from each other. We had dinner in the village and then agreed to meet on the plaza at 7:30 a.m. to walk together the next day.

Being the spreadsheet pilgrim that I am, the next morning, I was at the rendezvous location at 7:20 a.m. I got a cup of coffee and waited for Evelyn. Seven thirty came and went … seven forty-five, and still no Evelyn. I thought, *Well, perhaps a couple of days of walking with Steve Walther was enough and she decided to go her own way.* Sad and disappointed, I headed out onto the Camino walking solo. I eventually met a German pilgrim, Sascha, and the day's Camino eventually brought us to a fork in the road. The right fork followed the highway, and the left fork ducked off into a forest and followed a small stream for most of the next several hours. We met a Portuguese husband-and-wife couple that were mushroom hunters. They gave us a peek at their bounty and shared the names of the mushrooms in their basket. We walked with an elderly sheepherder and his flock of sheep. Like so many off-color jokes start, the sheep, the shepherd, the German, and the American walked together for the last few kilometers before walking into O Porriño. Sascha and I stopped in a café for a strong dose of Spanish caffeine, and while sitting, I checked my phone.

A string of texts from Evelyn popped up: "Where are you? Did you leave? Are you in O Porriño?"

Evelyn had overslept or it may have been because crossing from Portugal into Spain, there is an hour time change and maybe one of us were off on the correct time. In any event, she headed onto the Camino after I had left. On that particular route, the internet coverage was poor and she didn't see my texts in the morning and I didn't see her texts regarding her waking up late. Evelyn walked by herself that day and when she came to the fork in the trail, she unfortunately, took the right fork and walked the last several hours on the side of a highway with trucks zooming inches away from her head and backpack. She had just arrived in O Porriño and sent me her location. Sascha decided to keep walking and headed back out onto the Camino. I walked to the center of O Porriño and found a very sad and frazzled Evelyn.

We sat in a café off of a small plaza and ordered pulpo and beers. I shared my adventure with Sascha, the mushroom hunters and walking in and among a flock of sheep for several wonderful miles of pathway that followed along the shaded stream bank and all the way into the outskirts of the village. She, on the other hand, shared her dreadful, life-threatening accounts of the trucks, buses, and traffic zooming by her as she marched on the narrow shoulder of the asphalt highway. The pulpo and beer helped calm Evelyn, and we agreed to make sure we walked together the next morning.

As we finished our wonderful Galician delicacy of pulpo (octopus) topped with olive oil, paprika, and a side of incredible slices of baguette, we both relaxed and talked about our next day. After some conversation, we both sat in silence for a few minutes. I put my hand into my jacket pocket and realized that I had the second Manitas de Mocho in my pocket.

I leaned into Evelyn and said, "Have you heard the story of Mocho and of his Manitas de Mocho?"

She had not, so I started in with the same story told to me by Andrea in that small dark refugio up top El Paseo de Palos on the Primitivo Route. She listened to the story, and as I came to the last part of the story, I leaned in and reached out to her hand with the Manitas de Mocho in my hand.

Evelyn was immediately overcome with happiness. She began to cry. She said that I had no idea how much she really needed that in that very moment. Immediately, all of that day's troubles were now behind her. Back to the old saying, "Goose bumps are God telling us to pay attention," this was another moment of Camino magic that I was so blessed and fortunate that this time, I was able to be on the giving end of that magic!

Evelyn with her new Manita de Mocho

The year after my Camino on the Portuguese Central Route, I walked the Coastal Route up to Caminha and then cut inland back to the Central route in Valenca/Tui and up to Pontevedra and the Spiritual Variant. Since my visit and tour with Guilherme in Braga, he had actually moved to Santiago. When I walked into Obradoiro Square in front of the Cathedral de Santiago de Compostela, Guilherme was there with a big hug to meet me and welcome me home to Santiago.

Guilgerme's greating in Santiago

Another pilgrim legend, Leigh Brennan, had also moved to Santiago full-time since my last visit. Leigh is the host of the much-loved podcast, *The Camino Café* and *Good Morning, Santiago*. She fell in love with the Camino after walking her first pilgrimage on the Camino Frances route in 2019. She now broadcasts her *Camino Café* show from the heart of Santiago's old town. She interviews pilgrims and discussions on all things Camino and also highlights the current "happenings and vibes" of the astonishing city of Santiago. Leigh joined Guilherme and me and most of our Spiritual Variant boat crew for our arrival group dinner on the night that we arrived in Santiago.

We broke bread, drank wine, and basked in the wonderful warm feeling of both finishing the journey and reuniting with old friends. The end of a Camino is bittersweet, with the widest smiles that ebb and flow with occasional tears, knowing that many of these people that we have shared so much of our selves with we may never see again. We retold stories of our Camino and laughed a lot. The last night together is always powerfully enchanting and so very special. I thought to myself that I sure wish I had a few Manitas de Mocho to share with my fellow pilgrims that certainly lived up to the sentiment that Mocho himself loved so much about the heart of pilgrims.

Guilherme is very well connected with the various Camino associations and groups. At our dinner, I asked him if he was able to get any more Manitas de Mocho? He said that he may be able to get me a few before I left Santiago. Over the next few days, Guilherme shared that he was still working on "something" that would be even better than receiving a few manitas. I waited in anticipation.

On my last night in Santiago, Guilherme and I had dinner in the city center, and later we met with Leigh and her friend, Patti. Guilherme left us for a meeting that he had to attend, but said that when he called later, be ready to go quickly to meet him "somewhere." Off he went.

Leigh, Patti, and I visited with another mutual friend of ours, Juan Carlos the artist in his gallery. Juan Carlos was sharing his thoughts on what it means to be a pilgrim and all of the wonderful things he's experienced living in Santiago for over thirty years when Leigh's phone rang. It was Guilherme with an address and strict instructions: "Get here *now!*"

We ran out of the gallery and through the city center to a small bar just outside of the old town. We entered the bar to find Guilherme and his friend Maria sitting at a table with an elderly man…*It was Mocho!*

The Legend, Mocho!

Mocho is a nickname for Jose Sanchis. After first hearing of his story in that refugio atop the mountain pass on the Camino Primitive, I have told and retold the legend of Mocho countless times. Having him right there sitting in front of me was surreal. It was like sitting with Joe DiMaggio, Tom Hanks, and Mother Teresa all at the same time!

And per his legend, he lived up to the hype. He spent about thirty minutes with us over a beer and asking us questions. Questions such as, "Why do you walk the Camino?" "Why is it important to you?" "What have you learned about yourself?" Being the Camino geek that I am, I was in heaven and in the presence of so much good juju that I had a hard time finding my words to talk to Mr. Sanchis/Mocho. And for those of you that have spent any time with me at all, you know that finding my words is perhaps my superpower to the point that "Steve is best in small doses!"

Meeting Mocho

Meeting Mocho and spending time with maybe the most famous pilgrim on the Camino since Martin Sheen, Shirley McClain, or St. Frances himself walked the Camino will forever be one of my happiest and most special moments in life. Regarding my daughter and trying to share the magic that happens on the Camino, after our visit with Mocho, on my walk back to where I was staying, I called Dani on the phone and said, "You're never going to guess who I just met in Santiago..."

Chapter

21

Tell Me about Your Little Hike

El Camino Primitivo

One of the most difficult things for me is to attempt to describe and explain what El Camino de Santiago is and what it is not. That seems simple, but let's give it a try... El Camino de Santiago is a religious pilgrimage; but most of the pilgrims are not doing it for religious reasons. El Camino is indeed a hike; but the Camino is not really a hike at all. The pilgrimage is called the Camino, or the Way. However, there is not really one way but, rather, many different routes that all culminate at the center, like the hub of a wagon wheel, in Santiago de Compostela.

All roads lead to Santiago!

A person may set out on the Camino as a holiday but return forever a changed person. Regarding culture, no better way to learn a culture than to be fully immersed in all aspects of it from language, food, drink, accommodations, and by walking through farms and villages in which locals are going about their daily routines as we walk through their lives in real time. It's one thing to read about history and culture, but something altogether different when one experiences it by walking through it. Smelling it. Touching it. Tasting it. Living it.

I've heard people refer to El Camino as the best "slow tourism" vacation one could take. The more I think about that statement, the more I believe that the "slow" in slow tourism is the most valuable aspect of walking a Camino and why so many pilgrims long to return once they have completed their first. The Camino provides time to think, unplug from the world. In our fast-paced world, we neglect finding quiet and time for contemplation. With emails, texting, Grubhub, home gyms, and On Demand "everything," we have forgotten how to just slow down and visit with people in conversation. I have very fond memories of spending time with my grandparents and how often that time was spent just "visiting." Friends would stop by Grandma and Grandpa's house and visit. Updates on the neighbor's children trying to get into a top university. Commentary on current events or a recent ball game while drinking a lemonade sitting around the table or out on the back patio were memories of a better time. Some of my favorite conversations and learning opportunities came from just listening to the conversations of those "visits." The Camino provides us with a chance and unique format from which to connect with people while on a long walk and time to just visit. As humans, we are all yearning for this.

The walking pace allows pilgrims to take note of the beautiful landscapes that may be missed if traveling by car, bus, or train. The sound of the cowbell ringing from a distant hillside. The clicking of walking sticks in the morning fog tapping on cobblestoned street that have been walked on for a thousand years by pilgrims experiencing the same sights, smells. and magic as you. The smell of the country, a wafting mixture of pine, flora, and fauna ... mostly of the manure-producing variety that line the Camino paths and often appear to be spectators watching you on your journey, when in reality, it is you taking notice of them.

Panadería, freshly baked bread

The early morning aroma of warm bread baking for the customary tostada con mermelada served with the very robust coffee that has been roasted, with sugar to take some of the bitterness away. Freshly turned warm soil and flowering fruit trees create another dimension that cannot be replicated in a guidebook. Walking through a village and down the aisles of a public meat and fish market can be such a lasting memory in both experience and smell that those of us living in a more modern urban setting long for this form of a simpler time that still exists in such places.

The pilgrim wakes up early in the morning. Sets out from their albergue with all of their essential belongings in a backpack, and steps into a path without judgment. None of the comforts of home are necessary. For many, a sense of "decluttering" their lives is felt by pilgrims upon reentering their "post-Camino" lives. We don't really need all the "stuff" to be happy. The Camino mantra of "Walk, eat, drink, sleep, repeat," is really that simple.

The Camino is an opportunity to be alone in thought or be joined by others that are happy to share in your thoughts. In my case, other than one Camino with my daughter, I have left alone but returned with lifelong friends that I may have only met briefly. We may have shared a story, a coffee, a meal, but most importantly, we created a feeling and memory that makes us want to be a better person. That wanting to do good and be good seems to be a universal takeaway from most pilgrims that I have spoken with after they have walked for a time on a Camino.

Pilgrims

One of my favorite quotes by one of my favorite people, John Muir:

"Hiking—I don't like either the word or the thing. People ought to saunter in the mountains, not hike! Do you know the origin of that word 'saunter'? It's a beautiful word. Away back in the Middle Ages, people used to go on pilgrimages to the Holy Land, and when people in the villages through which they passed asked where they were going, they would reply, 'A la sainte terre' ('To the Holy Land'). And so they became known as sainte-terre-ers, or saunterers. Now these mountains are our Holy Land, and we ought to saunter through them reverently, not 'hike' through them."

Chapter

22

Shown the Way by a Blind Man

Somewhere near Melide on the French Route, our small Camino family walked into a village near the end of the day. We stepped into a café with a nice patio out front for a beer and tapas. The two Canadian women and I had reserved rooms in a rural house a few kilometers off of the Camino, and the owners of the house had sent us a number to call when we arrived in the village and they would come and escort us out to their house out in the country for dinner and our stay in their home.

While we waited for our ride out to the house, we joined another table of pilgrims and shared stories of our adventures of that day on the trail. Some of the pilgrims in my group had met this group in the days or weeks prior, and they were all happy to be reunited once again. The "newbies" introduced ourselves and where we were from. Two of the pilgrims, a man and a woman, were British and had walked with my "family" previously somewhere along the way. The Brits sat on my side of the table at the far end. They were all very lovely, and we joked, drank a few cold beers, and had a great time. The man's name was Tom. Tom told some funny accounts of their Camino, and we all laughed and laughed. Before too long, our ride arrived, and we said goodbye and left our new friends where we had met them, and we rode off to our home for the night in the country.

The very next afternoon, we caught up with our friends from the café from the day before. As I approached Tom and his friend, I said, "Buen Camino! How are you pilgrims doing today?"

Tom replied simply, "Buen Camino."

No emotion. No smile or "Great to see you, Steve, it was fun last night at the café." Nothing.

After we passed their group and marched on, I turned to Janette, who knew Tom from earlier in the Camino, and I said, "That was weird. Tom acted as though he had never seen us before."

Janette said, "Well … that's because he hasn't seen us before."

"We had beers, told stories, joked, and laughed just yesterday?"

Janette then told Tom's story: "Tom has a rare eye disease that has caused him to go blind very quickly. He wanted to do the Camino before he went totally blind and set out from St. Jean Pied de Port by himself walking the Camino with very little sight in hopes of finishing before he went completely blind. He met the woman who was walking with him on the first day over the Pyrenees and she has walked with him since they first met on the Camino."

Janette said that the woman had told her that his sight had gotten much worse in the four weeks they had been walking.

Pilgrims talk about finding "Camino Angels" that seem to appear when they need them the most… Well, Tom certainly found his angel. I never saw Tom or his angel again on the Camino, but I think of them both often. When I'm walking or struggling with something, I think about the faith and courage it took for Tom to set out on a path while struggling with the realization that his sight would be gone forever. While at the same time, the selflessness of his angel and what she did for Tom, a person whom she had never met before. She may not have been an angel when she set out on the Camino, but she certainly was an angel on the Camino. Without question, her path to heaven will not require any standing in lines… she goes right through!

"For it is in giving that we receive" (St. Francis of Assisi).

Side note, under the Who's Who of famous Camino pilgrims: St Francis of Assisi walked El Camino de Santiago de Compostela!

Chapter

23

A Mountain of Stones: Carrying the Weight of Those We Love

Memorial Stones

On El Camino Frances, there is a landmark that transcends a dot on the map or a paragraph in the guidebook. The Cruz de Ferro (the Iron Cross) is located on the Camino between Manjarín and Foncebadón. The cross is a wooden post with a large iron cross on top. If you were to just look at the cross without knowing any more about the tradition and history, it would still be an interesting site to behold. But the magic of the Iron Cross is in that very history and tradition. Its exact origin is unknown. Some believe the first cross was erected to mark the road when it snows and the Camino lost to pilgrims searching for the route.

Others have the wooden post's start dating back to Celtic times marking the prehistoric trails that followed the earth's ley lines. Without knowing when the first marker was placed on the hill, we do know that in the early eleventh century, an abbot named Gaucelmo placed a cross on the hilltop to mark the way to lodging in the villages below. Later, seasonal farm workers coming to work the harvest would walk the path from the surrounding kingdoms and pass by the cross on their way to Galicia. It is believed they first started the tradition of placing a stone from their journey at the base of the pole and the cross.

That traditional continues today with pilgrims on El Camino de Santiago. Pilgrims bring a stone or memento from home to leave at the cross. It signifies the laying down of one's burdens, a prayer for someone in need, to memorialize a loved one before receiving a blessing in Santiago at the end of the Camino. It is customary to say the traditional pilgrims' prayer at the Cruz de Ferro when placing your stone: *"Lord, may this stone, a symbol of my efforts on the pilgrimage that I lay at the foot of the cross, weigh the balance in favor of my good deeds someday when the deeds of my life are judged. Let it be so."*

Prayer stones along El Camino

After years of pebble-placing pilgrims passing by the Cruz de Ferro, it has become quite the site with a mountain of stones surrounding the cross on top of the pass. The pebbles and stones placed on top of the hill have actually grown into a mountain of stones and something to behold. The pure symbolism of the quantity of stones/burdens left in this place creates emotions of both somberness and joy. A sense of celebration and quiet reflection are felt.

On his podcast, *My Camino: The Podcast*, Dan Mullins interviewed an author named Rebekah Scott. Rebekah is a pilgrim, an author, a blogger, and a spiritual powerhouse living in a small village on the French Route itself. Rebekah and her husband, Patrick, offer to pilgrims two rooms in their old farmhouse a night's food and lodging in exchange for whatever the pilgrim wants to give. Regarding her guests, in her book, she described these pilgrims and those that pass through as "nuns, bums, Oxford dons, mystics, fugitives, hippies, and lunatics, as well as greyhounds, barn cats, roosters, and donkeys. Most moved on after a day or two, but some came to stay."

During Dan's interview with Rebekah, she said something that perhaps summed up the Camino so perfectly when considering places like the Cruz de Ferro. Rebekah said, "The Camino had some serious *juju* that is a feeling much more than a place."

The spirituality of the Camino comes to those that may not have been looking for that aspect of their Camino experience. It manifests itself in many different ways, but that feeling, that juju, is real. The magic is real. Walking is therapeutic. Walking helps us forget about life's struggles. The simplicity of the Camino allows pilgrims to let go of things that really aren't that important and focus on things that are.

The sentiment of the Cruz de Ferro and of walking in memory or in thought of others is not singular to that one hilltop along the French Route. Along all of the different Caminos that I have walked, I have seen stones placed in peaceful places, atop the Camino waymarkers or on stone walls and fences. I often find myself reflecting on people that I know back home that are struggling with personal pain or loss. It is easy to pick up a stone along the Camino and walk with that stone in hand, thinking about that person. To pray for that person. And then I leave their stone in a unique place for others to walk by and see my special stone, knowing that it was left in memory of something that perhaps could use a prayer or some of Rebekah's "serious juju!"

Remembering

I have shared this aspect of the Camino with people back home before leaving on a pilgrimage—people that were dealing with something that I know was causing grief, pain, or sorrow in their lives. Then, once out on the trail, when I find the perfect stone, I walk with it for a while. When I see a special place that seems fitting for that person, I leave their stone. I take a photo of their stone poised along the ancient pilgrimage in a position of significance and text a photo to that person with a simple note, "You are with me, and I am with you back home."

Chapter

24

Welcome to My Camino
Pity Party

As I have repeated over and over, perhaps my favorite aspects of the Camino are the pilgrims themselves. I have learned so much about the world, perspective, and about myself by walking, breaking bread, and sharing the Camino with pilgrims. Preparing for each pilgrimage, I get most excited about the new friends that I am going to meet on my next adventure. The lifelong friends that I met on previous Caminos are more than just acquaintances. We have a connection that cannot be replicated anywhere else. We share the difficulties, the joy, the pain, the life-changing conversations. We open ourselves and our hearts, the good and challenges.

Everybody has a story if you take the time to listen. There is something to learn from everybody and their experiences. These connections are part of the magic that I yearn for when not on the Camino. This feeling is the reason why most pilgrims are already planning their next pilgrimage before they finish the one they are currently walking!

On my third Camino, I walked the Portuguese Central Route from Porto, Portugal. I enjoyed a couple of days in Porto before heading out on the Camino solo. Porto is an incredible city full of history, culture, and *port* wine! I encourage anybody thinking about walking this route to take the time to explore Porto before heading out on the Camino itself.

During COVID, all the albergues and hotels were closed. Over the summer of 2021, they started to open back up, but with strict regulations. Albergues were limited on the number of beds in each room and the six-foot separation rules dictated that common areas did not have the same culture and sense of community that we enjoyed pre-pandemic. With the limited options for sleeping, I booked ahead out of fear of not finding arrangements in the smaller villages.

I left Porto in November of 2021 by myself. I like walking in the late fall because it is typically cooler and less crowded. The less-crowded aspect is both a blessing and a curse. On this particular Camino, I saw only a handful of pilgrims on my first three days out of Porto. As mentioned, out of my concern of not finding rooms, I booked most of my stays in advance. It turned out that my spreadsheeting aptitude was overplayed, as I was the only pilgrim in the first two places that I stayed. For those that know me know that I am very gregarious. That is perhaps is the biggest understatement of this entire book! My superpower is that I will talk to anybody about anything in any situation. After three days of mostly walking in silence, a bit of anxiety started to set in.

On my third night, I stayed in a wonderful old farmhouse that was made into a country inn. I had an incredible room, and the property included a beautiful garden, patio, and a very old-world kitchen that was available for me to use to cook my dinner. The farmhouse was about one kilometer from a small village that consisted of a tractor repair shop, a gas station, and a corner business that functioned as the town gathering place. It was a bar, restaurant, and market all in one. The local farmers and their families crowded around the bar and the small tables scattered throughout the white-tiled establishment. A soccer/futbol game blared from the televisions that were hoisted up in each of the corners and behind the bar. A small door at the side of the bar led into the small market that was stocked with the most basics of Spanish staples: bread, wine, beer, water, a few vegetables, apples, oranges, various sizes and flavors of cured meats, cheese, olive oil, bags of pasta, and various canned goods lined a few shelves.

I rewarded myself with a beer at the bar and as the patrons watched the soccer game in suspense, I enjoyed watching them and at least attempting to be a part of something ... anything! I don't really like soccer, but it was glorious just to be around people after a couple of days of walking alone and in silence. After my beer, I bought a bottle of wine, a loaf of freshly baked bread, a package of chorizo, cheese, and the juiciest giant red tomato and headed back to the inn and its large kitchen. I sat at the heavy large old dark oak table with my enormous chorizo, cheese, and tomato sandwich and bottle of wine and called home to check in with my wife, Maria Eugenia.

Feeling a little bit sad and lonely having been anticipating walking with other pilgrims, I was throwing myself a bit of a pity party. I shared with Maria Eugenia that I was a bit disappointed with this Camino due to the lack of pilgrims. She said, "Maybe that is God's plan for you on the Camino … to make it about you and to reflect and think about what you are doing?"

She was spot on! From that moment forward, my demeanor changed, and I no longer looked for what was not there and embraced what was right there in front of me. The Camino provides. It took my wife back home to remind me of what is really important. The next day, the sun was out, and the birds seemed to chirp a little louder. For the first fifteen miles that day, I walked in deep thought and with a smile. I thought about friends back home that were going through some health issues. The day before I set out for Portugal, three of the boys I grew up with lost their dad. He was a like a father to many in our town. I was able to walk with them on that day and enjoy their company in memory and with a pep in my step. Be thankful for what you have and worry less about what you don't.

And with this valuable lesson and time spent in thought and reflection, the very next day, I met the pilgrims that went on to become my Camino family, who I completed the rest of the walk with. I really believe that what Maria Eugenia had told me made my Camino play out in this order. Whether truly serendipitous or actual divine intervention, it doesn't really matter. The Camino eventually gave me my pilgrim family and reminded me that I am alive, with purpose and, with each step, a sense of accomplishment.

Why walk the Camino? The Camino is affirmation that life is actually pretty awesome. The Way gives significance to your relationship to a Higher Power, whether that is God or nature. It also reminds us to be grateful for what we have rather than dwelling on what we don't.

Chapter

25

Manolo, the Jean Walker

On the Camino Primitivo, Dani and I left Oviedo on a June 4, 2019. The Primitivo is perhaps the most beautiful of all the Caminos. Also, it is one of the most challenging, from the rocky climbs and descents through valleys and across rivers and mountains. The two of us headed out at the crack of light each of the first few mornings fueled by strong Spanish coffee and, of course, using our headlamps as our guiding torch into the morning darkness. Never again Juhwan, never again!

Each of the first several mornings, at precisely 10:00 a.m., a skinny Spanish man in his mid-forties, wearing jeans, a button-down shirt, dress shoes, Coke-bottle glasses, and a small canvas knapsack came flying up the trail from behind, passed us and left us in the dust. Each and every time, after our ceremonious "Buen Camino y buenos dias," he disappeared, becoming smaller and smaller as he zipped up the trail just short of an all-out jog until he disappeared on the horizon.

The first time he motored past us, Dani asked, "What the hell was that?"

The second time, she stated, "Huh, I hadn't thought of wearing penny loafers and jeans. They don't seem to slow him down any!"

Dani later gave the fast dressed-up pilgrim the handle "the Jean Walker." We continued to see the Jean Walker each morning at about ten o'clock, and eventually became our Camino alarm reminder that it was time to start looking for a place to stop for the "pilgrim's second breakfast!"

In an earlier chapter, I mentioned Bea and Laura, the two peregrinas from Cadiz. After a long and beautiful walk from the ancient city of Lugo, we stopped in a small village called Ferreira for refreshments. We were joined by other pilgrims, and we shared stories, rested our legs, and thought about where we would eat dinner that evening. And then it happened. Dani leaned over to me and said, "There he is, Dad!"

I asked, "Who?"

"The Jean Walker," she said softly and out of the side of her mouth.

There in a red plastic chair sat the man himself, the Jean Walker.

I leaned over to Laura and asked her, "Have you guys noticed this guy over there on your daily walks?" as I motioned with my head signaling the direction that I wanted her to look.

Laura turned to see who I was signaling her to identify. She quickly said, "Oh, you mean the Late for Mass Pilgrim!"

Bea and Laura had dubbed him the "Late for Mass" walker to our "Jean Walker."

The "Jean Walker/Late for Mass Pilgrim" sat by himself at a small table behind our large group.

After my questioning of Laura regarding this unusual pilgrim, she shrugged and called out, "Hey you! Yes, you ... there."

The man shrugged and pointed to himself in a questioning acknowledgment. She said, "Yes, you."

She asked, "What's your story?"

He said, "What do you mean?"

"Well, you are walking the Camino as though you were late for Mass!"

He then leaned back and began to tell his story. He said that he had lived in Oviedo his whole life. Pilgrims were always a part of growing up in Oviedo, but he had never walked the Camino. He said that on the night before he left, he was down at the corner bar having a drink with a friend. His friend confided in him that in the morning, he was going to walk the Camino de Santiago. Manolo said that he would sure like to join him; however, he did not have any gear for the journey. His friend told him that he didn't either, but he knew a guy in the first village after a day's walk after Oviedo that had everything they would need—backpack, rain gear, hiking boots, walking poles, etc.

After another cup of courage, Manolo agreed to join his friend on this life changing adventure, and they both agreed to leave the bar immediately to go home and get a good night's sleep before heading out early in the morning on the first day of their walk on the "Primitivo" Camino, the first Camino route in the history of all Caminos first walked on by King Alfonso II in the ninth century.

Manolo headed home from the bar and announced to his mother and sister that he was leaving in the morning on El Camino. Both his sister and his mother responded by stating that he wouldn't finish and that he never finished anything. They said he would and could never complete the famed Camino de Santiago. Manolo was in his mid-forties, lived at home with his mother, and was a construction laborer. He had never really left Oviedo and, apparently, never considered leaving, let alone walking out of the only home he had ever known. He affirmed that yes, he was going to do it and he was leaving at seven o'clock that very next morning.

In the morning, Manolo met his friend at the prearranged starting point, and off they walked toward the first town of Grado where they would meet with the friend with the hiking gear. That first day out of Oviedo is not a particular long walk, maybe sixteen miles or so. But there are a few ascents and descents that do get the lungs working and the heart pumping pretty good. The two amigos left Oviedo with high hopes of life-changing adventure and accomplishment and dressed much as they were when they had concocted this plan the night before in the pub.

Manolo was wearing jeans, a button-down shirt, and loafers; and he had a small canvas knapsack that included some underwear, a couple of tee shirts and a pair of flip-flops. The two exhausted rookie pilgrims limped into Grado in their nontraditional hiking setups and came to the center of town and stopped.

Standing at the corner of an intersection, the friend announced, "The Camino Sucks, I'm out!"

At that very moment, a cab pulled up to where they were standing, and the friend got into the cab and headed back to Oviedo! Manolo said, "But what about the hiking gear? You can't just leave me here!"

The friend had already closed the taxi door and headed home before Manolo could do much of anything. He explained to us that he just stood there for a few minutes, uncertain of what do to next. He thought about what his mother and his sister had told him: "You never finish anything, and you'll be back in a day."

He knew that he could not go home. He had to finish what he set out to do. So in his Late for Mass outfit and with determination to finish, he was now a full-fledged pilgrim and committed to walking the rest of the way.

It was at that time that Manolo joined our Camino family, and he became, by far, the most interesting pilgrim that I have yet to walk with. And when I say interesting, I mean from an entertainment perspective. Walking the Camino with my daughter and Manolo was pure joy in the sense that everything to them both was new. The experience, interaction with other pilgrims, and the commitment to something bigger than themselves made their journey my happiness.

We learned later that Manolo's pattern of passing us at ten o'clock each morning after we had walked for a few hours was because he was not an early riser. It seemed that we spent nearly as much time waiting for Manolo than we did actually walking with Manolo. But with that aside, he was a welcome addition to our group, and may even be the final piece of our ensemble of the Island of Misfit Toys!

Bea and Laura both took it upon themselves to be Manolo's motherly figures on the Camino. They helped him order meals, ensured he didn't stray onto the wrong trail, found albergues for him to stay, and, most importantly, made sure he was inside the albergues before the door locking curfew had him locked out and sleeping on the street. Manolo was simple. Not simpleminded, but just simple. He had not experienced much of the world outside of the Spanish state of Asturias. He was a good son and checked in with his mother several times a day as we walked.

Bea, Laura & Manolo After more comfortable clothes were found on El Camino

On one particular morning, in a village somewhere between Melide and O Pedrouzo, we stayed in a small village. That night, everybody turned in early except for Manolo and me. We stayed down at the pub taste-testing the local refreshments, and minutes before the doors were locking at the albergue, we happened to notice what time it was and rushed back to our rooms for the night. Bea, Laura, and Manolo were in one albergue and Dani and I were in another one up the road. We had all agreed the night before to meet for breakfast at a café that was on the way out of the village.

That next morning, we all met for breakfast except for Manolo. He was nowhere to be found. I told Bea and Laura that I had seen him go into the albergue at eleven the night before, but after that, no idea where he might be. We ordered breakfast and enjoyed our coffee all while wondering what happened to Manolo. Bea said that there had been a big commotion during the night in the albergue. She said that in the middle of the night, a young Asian woman woke up screaming that there was a man trying to get into her bunk bed. The man apparently got up and ran out of the room and then out of the albergue altogether. She said that after a few minutes, it got quiet again and everybody went back to sleep.

A few minutes later, Manolo stumbled in the front door with his hair all out of sorts and looking a bit haggard. We all said in unison, "Manolo, where in the hell have you been?"

He plopped himself down, let out a long sigh, and said, "Last night, I climbed up into the top bunk and went to sleep. In the middle of the night, my phone charger slipped between the bed frame and the mattress and down onto the mattress and next to the sleeping pilgrim below me. I didn't want to wake her, so I climbed down and carefully reached over her, attempting to get my charger that had wedged down between her, the mattress, and the wall. As I straddled over her trying to get the charger very slowly and quietly, she woke up and started screaming! Then I started screaming! I grabbed my charger, jumped back into my bunk, and she continued screaming in some kind of language that I didn't understand. She went absolutely crazy and wouldn't stop yelling at me. I grabbed by bag, charger, shoes, and headed out the front door of the albergue, which locked behind me when the door closed. I then walked down to the plaza and slept the rest of the night on a bench. I didn't sleep very much. Geez, that lady was crazy!"

We all just sat there listening to his story, compared to what Bea and Laura had experienced from their perspective, and especially not knowing that the man was *our* Manolo!

In her motherly way, Bea said to Manolo, "You know, Manolo, maybe that girl wasn't crazy. It was just that you scared her with her opening her eyes from a deep sleep to find a man straddled over her in her bed?"

Manolo replied, "Maybe, but I just wanted to get my charger, and she didn't have to scream at me!"

My favorite part of that morning's tale of perception was the looks on Dani's face as she listened to the story unfold from that of a potential sexual predator attacker to the realization that it was just Manolo being Manolo and that fact that he was naive as to what had really happened. Dani and I walked with giant grins the rest of that morning; and several years later, Dani and I still smile when we think of Manolo.

At the end of our Primitivo, our Camino family all met at a very nice upscale, fancy restaurant in Santiago. I knew that Manolo didn't have extra money, and we noticed his reluctance when the plan was made to meet for dinner that night. We enjoyed a wonderful dinner and celebrated our adventure as our last night together came to an end. When nobody was paying attention, I paid Manolo's bill before they brought our bills to the table. I told him that Dani and I had had never met an Asturiano before and getting to know him was our pleasure. He was grateful, and after dinner, our group hit the streets of Santiago to celebrate our last night together.

In the morning, Dani and I made one more walk through the medieval city center and decided to have lunch in one of the cafes a few blocks from the cathedral before heading back to grab our bags and head to the airport. As we sat down, we saw Manolo walking past our table, and we signaled for him to join us for lunch. We again recapped our adventures from the previous weeks, and he was excited to catch a bus later that afternoon back to Oviedo to see his sister and his mother and report on all that he had accomplished in spite of their doubts. Manolo then said something that was so simple and perfect that I can still hear his words.

"You know, I've never met actual Americans before. You and Dani are much nicer than the Americans I know from television and the movies!"

With that, he gave us each a giant hug, and I could see that he was on the brink of tears. We said our goodbyes, and Manolo left our table, turned, and disappeared into the crowded street, and we never saw him again. After we finished our lunch, we motioned to the waiter in the international air-signing hand motion indicating that we were ready to pay. The waiter came over and said that the other gentleman had already paid the bill...

Last meal with Manolo

Chapter

26

A Cowboy Joined Us on the Camino

The Cowboy, Paul Walther

Pilgrims walk the Camino for many different reasons. Historically, pilgrims walked to Santiago for purely religious reasons. This is still true today, but the religious aspect is only one of the reasons. Some hike for a challenge. Others to get away from it all, unplug and connect with nature, and to walk with pilgrims from all over the world. While some are on El Camino because of changes in their lives, perhaps a change in careers, a breakup, or the loss of a loved one.

For me, the calling of El Camino has kind of been all of the above: Religious, spiritual, the connection with nature, the Spanish culture, connecting with others, and the physical challenge. That all changed halfway into our Camino Primitivo.

On June 11, 2019, exactly halfway into our hike, Dani and I learned that my father, her grandpa, had passed away after a long battle with kidney disease. We scrambled to figure out how to get home. After discussing this with my mother, she insisted that he would have wanted us to continue and not to quit. As difficult as it was, there probably was not a better place for Dani and me to be to remember, honor, and respect Dad than on El Camino de Santiago.

I really believed that he joined us on our Camino as another pilgrim at that point. Although I am quite certain that he was riding his horse rather than on foot, nonetheless, he was with us!

The focus and purpose of our Camino had changed. We talked about Grandpa. We told stories. Dani asked questions. I was able to cry, walk, cry, and walk some more. The Camino provided the space, time, and opportunity to grieve and remember. I am grateful for the wonderful pilgrims that we met on this Camino. They were both there for us and also able to give us space when they sensed we needed it.

I am most grateful that I was able to be there with Dani during this time. We had just celebrated her graduation with Grandpa the week prior back in Idaho, which made the timing of his passing even more poetic.

I still miss you, Dad. Without your lust for adventure and yearning to always be looking over the next mountain, around the next turn in the trail and hope in meeting your next friend, I would not have found El Camino de Santiago. You are always with us, and I am thankful for *everything*. Love you, Dad!

Chapter

27

Camino Angels

Ivy, Camino Angel

Somewhere on a rainy day on the Portuguese Camino, I walked down a narrow paved country road. The rhythm of the rain on my plastic poncho and walking sticks clicking on the road below made the wet walk more bearable as I hummed to myself and marched through the relentless Galician November rain. I was doing my best to keep the walking sticks in time with Paul Simon's "You Can Call me Al," when I saw another pilgrim walking slowly down the center of the road ahead of me. As I approached her to walk past, I offered the traditional greeting of "Buen Camino."

As I passed, I saw her face tucked inside of her poncho, and I could tell that she was crying. I asked if she was okay and needed help with anything. She simply replied, "My dad died."

I calmly asked, "Just now?"

Between a couple of sniffles, she replied, "No, in August."

It was November at that time. I stopped her and wrapped my arms around her in a big hug and said that it was okay to cry. I told her not to worry about her dad, and that he was right there with her on the trail, and that he was proud of her for taking on this adventure. I shared with her that I too had lost my dad and it was while I was walking another Camino.

We walked for a while farther before she finally said, "I'm sorry, I can't stop crying."

I told her, "You aren't crying, it's just that your face is rainy!"

She laughed, and her demeanor and mood began to change to a happier and lighter one. As often happens on the Camino, we eventually separated, and I did not see her for the rest of that day.

The next day, I ran into her again. She was in much better spirits, and I learned that her name was Ivy. (Yes, the same Ivy from the boat and Spiritual Variant). Ivy was from Taiwan, and contrary to our first encounter, she was a very strong and determined woman. I later learned that she was also an incredible artist. From photos she took during the day, she would do watercolor/pen-and-ink paintings in the evenings. Her work was spectacular. When I saw her the next day, she asked where I was going and asked me if I knew anything about the Spiritual Variant. I told her that I had read about and that I actually had an extra brochure on it if she wanted it. She took it, and we exchanged

WhatsApp numbers. (WhatsApp is a free phone application that allows you to make calls worldwide using your regular mobile phone number with other people that also have the app. It is a must on the Camino when communicating with other pilgrims and also for calling home.)

She was staying in that town where we were at that time, and I was going to walk up to the next town that afternoon. We said goodbye, and off I went to a small fishing village called Arcade. I had stayed in this town the year before and had a great time with my previous pilgrim family. I think the warm memories made me push forward to stay in that town.

Roger, an old friend of mine from my time living in Spain thirty years prior, sent me a message asking for a Camino update as to where I was and how it was going. I told him that I was in Arcade and about to have dinner. He responded that Arcade was famous for oysters and that I should have them while there. I told him that I would.

I walked down to the waterfront to the actual restaurant where I had eaten the year before with my previous group. I enjoyed a wonderful dinner, wine, and at the end, I thought that I better order a few oysters just so that I could take a picture and share with Roger that I had completed the task. I ate four oysters and then walked back to my room for the night.

I slept well and woke up with one of the shortest days on my trip the day ahead of me. It was raining off and on, but not unlike the days prior. I headed out from Arcade in the direction of Pontevedra. At first, it was just another wonderful day on the Camino. Then I started to feel weak. At one point, my wife, Maria Eugenia, called, and we had a nice visit. She shared what was happening on the home front, and I gave her my Camino status, and also that up until that day, I had felt great but, all of a sudden, began to feel weak and extremely fatigued. But nothing more than tired. She suggested that I slow down a bit, and I told her that on that particular day, it was the shortest leg of my entire Camino, so I should be able to rest.

Then it happened. Without going into graphic details, I left a lot of myself on the trailside that day walking between Arcade and Pontevedra. I'm thankful that it was only coming out of the top end and not the bottom end. But Arcade and those dang oysters had waged war on my stomach. Cramps and vomiting joined me on the Camino that day and accompanied me all the way into the great city of Pontevedra. I found my way to a small hotel in the city center and was barely able to check in and get up to my third-floor room and bathroom just in the nick of time. I dropped my pack, took off my wet shoes, socks, and clothes and just passed out.

A few hours later, my phone rang. It was Ivy. She asked if I was in Pontevedra, and if so, where was I staying? I told her that I had arrived and that I was already checked in to my room. She asked if the hotel had any free rooms, and I told her that I would check. I forced myself to sit up, put my clothes back on, and walk down the stairs to the elderly lady at the hotel front desk. I asked if they had any room left. She said that they had one left. I asked for her to hold the last one, that an Asian woman would be there shortly for that room, and then I returned upstairs. I phoned Ivy and told her that they were holding a room for her and texted her the address. She then asked, "Do they have laundry service?"

I paused, took a deep breath, and said that I wasn't sure but I couldn't find out for her. I explained that I was really sick and weak and unable to walk back downstairs to ask. I told her that I would like to join her for a walk around the city that night, but I wasn't going to move and that I probably wasn't going to be able to move the next morning either. She asked if I needed anything, and I told her, at that point, just rest.

A few moments later, the phone rang again. It was Ivy. When I answered the phone, it wasn't her but the voice of a Spanish woman. Ivy had checked into the hotel, then went out and looked for a pharmacy. She did not speak any Spanish, so she dialed my number and handed the phone to the pharmacist.

The pharmacist asked what my problem was. I explained my situation, and she said she would give something to Ivy to bring to me. A few moments later, Ivy knocked on my door with something for the stomach cramps, a probiotic, and a can of 7-Up.

She said, "Yesterday you were my angel. Today I am yours."

Chapter

28

The Camino Universe

My Camino Family 2022

By now, you've hopefully got a sense of the lifelong connection that pilgrims make along the Camino from my stories of bonds and friendships. Lifetime friendships are often forged out of a few days, a few hours, or even just few moments of conversations and shared experiences. These connections are global and can often be some of the most heartfelt, meaningful personal relationships that you'll cherish for the rest of your life.

One of the most interesting things that I've experienced is that these connections are not limited to people that you have met on the Camino. My Camino family continues to grow with pilgrims that I have met that I did not meet on the Camino itself. But through our shared passion and commitment to what we learned and experienced, we are able to continue the Camino spark through newfound friendships with our shared relationship with St. James and his little walkabout as our touchstone!

Guilherme & Leigh, Podcasting

I've previously mentioned my friends Guilherme and Leigh Brennon, who I met via their Camino podcasts. I brought them with me on my daily walks, listening to their words of wisdom, and learning from the pilgrims that they interviewed as I walked and prepared for my upcoming Caminos. I shared in their enthusiasm, warmth, and passion for all things Camino. Our virtual relationship eventually led to me meeting them both in real life, and I now consider both of them to be not only my Camino buddies but two of my closest friends who share the same yearning to better themselves and continue to glow in the pilgrim experience.

I had the good fortune of having had Dan Mullins ask to interview me after my first Camino and in his early years of doing his podcast. Perhaps more than anybody, Dan has become such a wonderful ambassador for El Camino de Santiago and for all pilgrims. His kindness and warm heart make it easy for all that follow his show to become his friend, even though most of us have not actually met Dan face-to-face. He is both a Camino father figure and also a friendly bloke to share a pint with over either a funny story or a profound, sincere story of faith and love. Dan is every Camino's favorite friend. And on top of that, he can sing and play the guitar amazingly as well!

Before my first Camino, I was getting my daily steps in on a local greenbelt path in my hometown of Eagle, Idaho. On that particular day, I was walking with my backpack and trying to wear in a new pair of hiking boots. As I passed by a guy sitting on a bench with bike leaning up against the end of the bench, he said, "What hike are you training for?"

I replied, "El Camino de Santiago."

He sat up and asked, "Have you read the book called *I'll Push You?*"

I told him that I hadn't and that I didn't know anything about it. He went on to tell me that it was the true story of two lifelong childhood friends, Patrick and Justin, who were actually from the Boise area. They grew up together from grammar school, high school, and, eventually, were even best men in each other's weddings. They both had good careers, had kids, their families traveled together, and life was going great. Then, very sadly, Justin developed a form of ALS. Patrick and his wife would fly down to Southern California, where Justin and his family lived, to help out the family when they could. On one of those trips, Justin told Patrick to check out a show he had recorded on the DVR. It was a Rick Steves's travel show featuring El Camino de Santiago. Justin said, "Isn't that something?"

Patrick said, "I'll push you!"

Without going into their story too much (please buy the book, watch the movie, download the audiobook—one of the most incredible stories of friendship, perseverance, and endurance ever written), from that point, they set off to do the Camino Frances with Justin in a special chair and with his best friend Patrick pushing him all the way from Saint-Jean-Pied-de-Port to Santiago de Compostela.

The man on the park bench introduced himself as Brent and said that he had a copy of the book that he would lend me. The next day, he dropped off the book in my office, and I started to read it. I eventually downloaded the audiobook version and listened to their adventure as I trained for my upcoming Camino.

Well, fast-forward a few years later. Back to Dan Mullins and his podcast. Dan sent me a note one day that read, "Don't you live in Eagle, Idaho? I just interviewed Patrick and Justin, they live in Eagle, Idaho."

I replied, "Yes, I do live in Eagle, Idaho, but I didn't know that was where they both lived. I do not know them."

Dan sent me their email addresses. I immediately sent Justin and Patrick a quick email introducing myself and thanking them for their wonderful book and for sharing their story on Dan's podcast. I asked if they would like to get together for lunch. They both quickly replied, and my timing could not have been worse… this was the early stages of the pandemic. Patrick and Justin both said that they would love to grab lunch, but they would prefer until this little pandemic thing cooled off a bit.

About a year later, I was walking down the sidewalk in our small town of Eagle, Idaho, and I saw a familiar-looking tall man walking next to another man in a powered wheelchair coming down the sidewalk ahead of me. I shouted out, "Hey, look, the 'I'll Push You' boys!"

We both laughed, and we then stopped at a local café and enjoyed lunch together. By watching them interact and talk to each other, I could quickly see that their friendship went far beyond buddies. Having caring, loving friends like Patrick and Justin are to each other is certainly something we can all aspire to and hope to find in our own lives. Their Camino spirit was probably the most profound that I have experienced. We enjoyed a very nice lunch and conversation. A few weeks later, joined by their incredible wives, they came over to our house, and Maria prepared a traditional Spanish meal, and we told stories and created memories that I will treasure for the rest of my life.

My introduction to Patrick and Justin came via a man on a park bench with an interest in the Camino, and eventually from another man in Australia that shared an email with me here in Idaho. The Camino juju is strong and seems to always put the right people together.

The story actually has one more layer that brings it all home. A few months ago, I was traveling for work and waiting for a flight to Atlanta in the Boise airport. I saw a lady with a backpack that had a Camino shell patch on the back. I approached her and asked if she was headed to the Camino. She said that she was, and I asked her which route she was walking.

We had a short conversation, and she told me that she was a bit nervous that she was going by herself and really didn't know that much about the Camino. Sondra was heading out on the Portuguese Route from Lisbon. She was flying from Boise to San Francisco, where she would have a long layover. I told her, while she was waiting, to quickly download a few podcasts to get some basic information. I shared with her Dan's, Guilherme's and Leigh's podcasts and told her to listen to them on her way to Lisbon. We shared email address and phone numbers, and I asked for her to please send me updates of her adventure.

Throughout her Camino, I followed Sondra with jealousy and admiration. As she approached Santiago, I learned via a Facebook post by Leigh Brennan that Dan Mullins was walking the Camino with his family and would be arriving in Santiago on the same day as Sondra. Dan was going to be performing a small concert in a local Santiago pub on that very night. I told Sondra that she *must* go and see Dan perform. I then told Leigh that a friend from Boise was walking in on the Portuguese route that day, and I had told her about the concert and asked for her to look for Sondra. Leigh sent me a text back: "Did Sondra walk into Santiago today with a pilgrim named Andrea?"

I sent Sondra a note: "Did you walk in today with a pilgrim named Andrea?"

Sondra: "Yes I did…?"

Back to Leigh: "Leigh, yes, she did walk in today with a pilgrim named Andrea!"

Leigh: "I am meeting your friend Sondra for dinner tonight with my friend Andrea!"

Such a small wonderful Camino world and universe! From the introduction of podcasts in the Boise airport to actually meeting all three of the people whose podcasts I recommended by chance without any connection from me was such a fun and incredible way for Sondra to finish her Camino and for me to continue with the perpetual Camino Pilgrim Perma-Grin!

Epilogue

The Camino de Santiago is such a wonderful story filled with fascinating history, inspiring people and an empowering feeling that affects the human spirit. Whatever one's reason for embarking on their Camino, they will return forever changed. Walking in the footsteps of so many that have made this pilgrimage can be felt with each and every step made today. The magic is real. The spirituality is real. The love is real.

The Camino de Santiago has become such an important centerpiece of my life. Walking has made an impact on my physical, mental, and spiritual health. I am a better person for it. The Camino has brought me inner peace and direction. The Camino has made me strive to be a better husband, father, son, brother, friend, and human being. It is interesting that by just wandering around, one can really find oneself.

Often with only an innocent "Buen Camino" as the opening dialogue, the pilgrims that I have met on the Camino have become such cherished treasures in my life. I am thankful for what I have learned from each and every one of them. I am grateful for the realization that from these inspiring people from all corners of the globe and from all walks of life the basic truth is that we are ultimately all the same. We all want to love and want to be loved. We long for hope and happiness. The Camino shows us how wonderful life actually is if we just make the time to enjoy it, see it, and embrace it.

I hold those that have made me a better person from our time on the Camino in a very special place in my heart and soul. Some of you I've met only over the course of a few hours. While with others, we continue to share adventures and seek guidance and a taste of that feeling of being the best versions of ourselves while on the Camino itself.

Janette, Brigitte, Eliceu, Robert, Juhwan, Emilio, Peter, and Linda from my first Camino on the Frances and onto Finisterre, you were my first Camino family, and you showed me how to be a pilgrim "our" way. And my daughter Danielle and the rest of our Camino Primitivo family—Bea, Laura, Manolo, Jose, Andrea, Antonio, Juan, Ismael, and Pauline—what a fun group of adventurers! Edyta, Antonio, Evelyn, and Sebastian, it would have been difficult to create such a unique ensemble anywhere else in the world. You four will forever be some of my favorite people on the Camino, and maybe even the planet! And last but not the least, my last Camino core family group, Team Piedra y Agua, Sergio, and Ivy—you both made the rain enjoyable and the wind unnoticeable. With your perseverance, the commandeering of a captain and the addition of Nadia brought us into Padron and Santiago in style! All of you are forever etched in my memory and heart.

And most of all, I want to give thanks to my beautiful bride, Maria Eugenia. You have shared so much of your culture with me and sacrificed so much to live so far away from it. I am eternally grateful for all that you give me and for the freedom of encouraging me to walk the Camino. There is no me without you. Te quiero, guapa!

I think the best way to close out *Sacred Blisters* is with a blessing given to Sergio, Ivy, and me by the nuns at the monastery in Armenteira. I can think of no better prayer than this one to leave you with the Camino spirit. Thank you for coming along on my Camino, and I hope that with these words and stories, you are inspired to create your own story and adventure on El Camino de Santiago de Compostela!

Buen Camino!

Monastery of Armenteira Blessing for the pilgrim

May the light and love of God bless and direct your steps.
May the roads rise up to meet you.
May you open your heart to silence.
And keep with gratitude and joyous remembrance of the good things that you have encountered.
May God carry you in his hands to the arms of St. James in Santiago.
And may you go back to your home full of light and joy.

146

Camino Family 2018

Camino Family 2019

Camino Family, Emilio, 2018

Camino Family 2021

Dad & Daughter, June 2019

Camino Family, 2022

About the Author

Steve Walther

Studying Geography and Art at Humboldt State University (now Cal Poly Humboldt), walking in perpetuity on El Camino de Santiago in Spain is obviously the only appropriate dream career for Steve Walther. Unfortunately, walking doesn't pay the bills and keep a pilgrim in vino and chorizo. When not walking on, dreaming about, or talking about the Camino, he works as a speaker and trainer for financial advisors, insurance agents, CPAs and estate planning attorneys.

Steve first lived in Spain after college in 1992 and fell in love with the people, culture and history of the Iberian Peninsula. So much so, that he married a wonderful Spaniard, Maria Eugenia, in Jerez de la Frontera in 1996. On one of his adventures exploring the Spanish countryside, he discovered Santiago de Compostela and was captivated. The story of one of Jesus' twelve apostles, St. James, coming to Spain and Portugal is a tale that like so many, fascinated him to the point that he had to walk the famed Camino de Santiago.

To date, Steve has walked four different Camino routes and is committed to walking as many as he can for as long as he is able. The life lessons learned on the Camino have changed Steve's life and perspective of the world. With this book, he hopes to share what he has learned and perhaps encourage readers to walk on their first of many Caminos.

Steve lives with this family in Eagle, Idaho. When not on the road, he enjoys hiking in the Idaho wilderness where you can usually find Steve on a trail with a fishing rod or camera in hand.

Ingram Content Group UK Ltd.
Milton Keynes UK
UKHW012045010523
421049UK00001B/69